WHEN TRAINS STOPPED IN DINORWIC

Eric and his dog, Jack, who followed him home from school one day in Hereford, 1912.

WHEN TRAINS STOPPED IN DINORWIC
The Story Of Eric Rhind

HAZEL FULFORD

Singing Shield Productions
THUNDER BAY, ONTARIO, 1990

Canadian Cataloguing in Publication Data

Fulford, Hazel, date
    When trains stopped in Dinorwic: the story of Eric Rhind
(A Northwestern Ontario heritage publication; 2)
Includes bibliographical references.
ISBN 0-9691717-2-2

1. Rhind, Eric. 2. Rhind family.   3. Frontier and pioneer life – Ontario – Dinorwic.
4. Immigrants – Ontario – Biography.   5. British – Ontario – Dinorwic – Biography.
I. Title.   II. Series.

FC3099.D56Z49 1990   971.3'112   C90-095450-7
F1059.5.D56F84 1990

When Trains Stopped In Dinorwic:
The Story Of Eric Rhind
by Hazel Fulford
Published by Singing Shield Productions
        104 Ray Blvd., Thunder Bay, Ontario, Canada P7B 4C4
        Telephone 807/344-8355

Design: Derek Chung Tiam Fook
Editor: Curtis Fahey
Printed and bound in Canada by Gagné Printing Ltd., Quebec
Back Cover Photograph: Bill Lindsay

Published with the assistance of The Ontario Heritage Foundation, (Ontario
Ministry of Culture and Communications), and of New Horizons, (National
Health and Welfare), through the RAPT Heritage Group.

This book is dedicated to my beloved grandchildren:

Calvin and Benjamin Fors,
Tegan, Nathan, Brennan and Calen Sacevich

Contents

ACKNOWLEDGMENTS

Several people deserve to be thanked for their contribution to this book. I am particularly indebted to my uncle, Eric Carden Rhind, and Daisy Wright,who is Eric's sister and my mother, for agreeing to share their memories with me in tape-recorded interviews. I would also like to thank Muriel Aboul-Atta, Eric's daughter, who helped to transcribe the tapes, and Milly Scollie, who confirmed Eric's childhood impressions of Intercity.

Elinor Barr gave valuable suggestions at every stage of the work. Mary Frost's helpful comments on the entire manuscript encouraged me to proceed with the final draft. George Campbell edited the pages dealing with railway operation. Bill Pendergrast taught me writing technique; his legacy, the Thunder Bay Writer's Guild, offered critical advice on the early chapters. Alex Finlayson of Dryden contributed the watercolour of the railway at Dinorwic (front end-paper) and permitted the use of his sketch of Quinn's Hotel. I thank my family for the use of period photographs, all the relatives and friends who helped in any way, and the RAPT Heritage Group for their support.

My husband, Don Fulford, made it possible to complete this project. Let me count the ways.

This is the tale of a life recollected; details may not coincide with other people's memories of the same events.

Hazel Fulford
Thunder Bay

PROLOGUE

"Let's begin in Dinorwic," my uncle said on a summer day in 1986 when we recorded his first tape. However, Eric Rhind's life did not begin in Dinorwic. And the impetus for this book did not originate with him either.

Two years earlier, Daisy Wright, who is Eric's sister and my mother, had agreed to make tapes about her years as a telegraph operator on the Canadian Pacific Railway (CPR) during both World Wars. My intention was to write about my mother's experiences as a telegrapher at various stations in Northwestern Ontario.

While we were making these tapes, the Wabigoon and District Historical Society was gathering material for a volume of regional and family histories. Eric's contribution was so well received that he wrote a longer memoir of the Rhinds for the benefit of his family and their descendants. And so I was led to reconsider my original plan.

Eric, eight years younger than Daisy, had grown up in Canada and was on the homestead when Daisy was working elsewhere. He knew the day-to-day life of the family after immigration; he also told anecdotes about his later working life. Yet he had spent his first eight years in Hereford, England, and had distinct memories of his childhood there. I decided to combine Eric's tales with Daisy's, using only that material of hers that he was involved with in some way.

My task at this point was to convince Eric that his life could actually be the subject of a book. However, in time, he agreed to record his memories and in 1986 we made eighteen tapes. I had made a list of questions as the basis for interviews, but I didn't adhere solely to this outline. Much was gained by allowing Eric to range freely over the years; some memories surfaced that had lain dormant for half a century.

Eric was uprooted at the age of eight when the Rhinds left England in the spring of 1914. His youth was interwoven with the fabric of Canadian history: the First World War, the age of steam on the CPR, the fur trade, the Trans-Canada Highway, the Red Lake gold rush, the Great Depression and the approach of the Second World War.

The family spent seven months at the Lakehead before settling in Dinorwic, an isolated hamlet on the railway line. Their first home in the village was an uninsulated shack heated by a wood stove. Eric and his ten-year-old brother, Gray, learned to split wood and haul water, to trap and fish, to carry their share of the desperate effort to survive.

But healthy children always find sources of amusement. Eric delighted in the characters living in and around the village, in their individual quirks and even in their animals. He absorbed the colour and tone of incidents that remained vivid in his memory. And now he recalled them for me.

By the time the tapes were transcribed I had decided to use five of Daisy's interviews and ten of Eric's, ending my story with his marriage. Eric was made the first-person narrator so I could begin with a child's eye view and also preserve the intimacy of the tapes. I pruned and rewrote the material so that it flowed easily.

As I wrote, I shared in the cosy, genteel life in Hereford, the rough ocean crossing and the first years of pioneering. I could see the long-awaited building of the homestead, hear the saws and hammers and the happy chatter as they moved into their own place.

The story begins in Hereford, with the question that still puzzles Eric: Why did the Rhinds move to Canada in the first place?

1

Fair Canada

I'm still not sure why we left England. Our family was in financial straits, but the reason for such a drastic move as immigration was never made clear.

My mother, Emma Eliza Hiles, was twenty-eight and my father, William Clarence Baikie Rhind, thirty-three when they married in 1890 and settled in Glenview, Mother's family home. By then Father was firmly anchored in his comfortable rut; it was too late to steer him into a great career. So Mother bossed him in small ways.

"A fellow can't even finish his pipe," he grumbled on Saturdays, torn from his book to dig in the garden or go to the fishmongers. He had become a dedicated reader during the years that his mother, Louisa, feared that any exertion might kill him. Her two daughters had died young. Then her husband, Dr. Samuel Rhind, developed pneumonia one dank November after making house calls in an open buggy. Tuberculosis followed and he died at forty-six. When her only son graduated in civil engineering three years later she decided that he needed a long sea voyage to preserve his health. He sailed with her to New Zealand, where they remained for several years. Then William fell ill; one of his symptoms was bleeding from the lungs.[1] He resigned his job as a railway station agent and returned to England with his mother. The weeks at sea were the peak of his life, recorded in a diary that he read again and again over the years. His other passions were the Church of England, mathematics and Dickens.

The class system at home paralleled that of society. Clarence, the eldest son, ranked next to our parents. His name entered the family through a paternal forefather who was a naval officer on a training ship in the eighteenth century. The Duke of Clarence, later King William IV,[2] was also on board; the two men became friends. From that time on the name Clarence was carried through the generations to my brother. He was fourteen when I was born

Eliza Rhind with sons Eric (left) and Gray at Hereford, c. 1909

on Valentine's Day, 1906; Bert was ten and Gray was two. The eldest daughter, Win, was thirteen. Daisy was an eight-year-old tomboy who spent her time with Bert. Since privilege was awarded according to rank, "Your turn will come" was the refrain of my childhood. I didn't believe that. Everyone in my home was older, taller and more clever than I.

By the time of my birth Mother had spent more than forty years in our house, which nestled beneath the Dinedor Hills in Hereford. The hills sloped down to a meadow that ran to our back garden. There were apple and pear trees here, vegetable plots and a stable. The vines of the climbing plum stitched themselves to the back wall of the house. The stone courtyard had a side entrance for tradesmen.

A row of apple trees separated our two gardens. The enormous rockery sprawled in front; here Win and Daisy hid coloured eggs at Easter for their little brothers. Stone walls separated us from our neighbours and the street. Our trees were sycamore, japonica and lilac. Virginia creeper embroidered the house and draped the front door like a shawl.

Inside, hall doors opened on a drawing-room furnished in rosewood, a dining-room where mahogany glowed under the gas chandelier, and a breakfast room. The fireplace in the breakfast room had a side oven and a kettle on the hob. A long staircase led to four large bedrooms and a dressing-room with bath. We no longer had a servant, but there was still a bell that could be sounded from the master bedroom.

There were two years in my childhood when Mother found time for the only child left at home. We roamed the countryside on sunny afternoons exploring Roman ruins and watching gypsies bake bread in outdoor ovens. Then I was six and the carefree days ended at the door of the Blue Coat School.

The headmaster of the Blue Coat School was Mr. Caldwell, a mild-looking runt with the heart of a sadist. The big boys were safe. I was the smallest child in the school, and so bruises and swollen hands were part of my life as a pupil.

The boys at the Blue Coat School marched into the big hall and lined up with hands over their eyes to recite the Lord's Prayer. The headmaster inspected finger nails. Dirty nails earned the offender a blow on the neck that cracked his stiff white collar. When sent from class to the headmaster you chose your own cane from a crock where they stood in water liberally laced with vinegar.

"Hands out, Rhind," he snarled one day. "Right out!" He swung the cane back over his puny shoulder and then hopped straight up and brought the cane down with a savage swish. I jumped back and the cane struck Mr. Caldwell's knee with a thwack! I was sure the noise could be heard all over the school. I ducked my head and covered my face as he lost all control and lashed out wildly with the cane. "Take that, you little brute! And that! I'll show you who is master here!"

When I limped home that day Bert had just come from his boxing lesson. His face turned scarlet when he saw me and he stormed out the door. Mr. Caldwell had a cut lip and a black eye the next day. He knew he had gone too far. There were no repercussions.

Our parents had solid middle-class backgrounds but no money. Dr. Rhind's had vanished in an investment scheme. The rental houses inherited by Mother, as the only child of Henry and Eliza Hiles, consumed more in taxes and upkeep than they earned. In 1914 new methods of accounting were established at Father's

The x in the front row marks Eric Rhind, smallest boy in the school.

firm and he lost his job at fifty-seven; there was no pension. At this point my brother Clarence, who had immigrated to Ontario, Canada, two years earlier, was working in a grain elevator at the Lakehead. One day we were told that we would be immigrating to the Lakehead as well. There was no explanation. "Little boys should be seen and not heard, Eric," the grown-ups always said.

Mother packed our clothes, a few keepsakes and a box of books in April 1914. Everything else was laid out all over the front garden. Our house was an empty shell.

Crown Derby china, chairs, tables and rugs disappeared through the front gate. I watched the stuffed owl that had perched on the hall coat rack. When Gray started school I talked to the owl. He never said, "Be quiet, Eric, I'm busy just now." To me he was one of the family. The burly auctioneer shouted, "Going, going, GONE!" The owl went for a shilling. My stomach flopped like a fish on the riverbank; my fingers itched to snatch my owl from the stranger. I tugged at Mother's hand, but there was no response. She stood stiff and straight as a flagpole, tears sliding down her cheeks. She didn't see Daisy and Bert aim a garden hose from behind the neighbour's wall and drench the people who were snatching up the Crown Derby. Where was Father? His height and his bushy moustache made him easy to spot. But not today. We didn't see him until the bellowing auctioneer was gone and the trampled grass bare.

The next day everyone but Win boarded the steamer *Royal George* at Southhampton. Twenty-two years old, Win had been settled in another home for some time as companion to an invalid lady.

While the others went to find our cabins Daisy and I stood at the rail. "Why did we have to leave?" I asked.

"A future for the boys," she said. "That's all they talk about – a future for the boys. What about *me*? My teacher said that Canada is full of savages." I had never seen her so cross. Perhaps she needed Bert beside her at that moment. He was eighteen, just two years older than Daisy. Both dark, headstrong and full of ginger, they had grown up as close as twins. She must have sensed that the end of life in Hereford was also the end of a special relationship.

As for me, I didn't care about the future. The deck tilted,

sank and rose again. My breakfast spewed over the rail and a pattern was set for the entire voyage. The Rhinds came from a line of naval men but in this family only Bert and Father had sea-legs. The rest of us could barely stagger from stuffy cabins below to the fresh air on deck. Sometimes Father carried me. We had to pass the engine room; a hot oily stench blasted into the corridor. We picked our way around blackened, sweaty men sprawled out having a smoke.

Soon after we left England I leaned on the rail to watch huge beasts plunging about in the ocean. I forgot my stomach and ran to Mother, calling, "Come and see the whales!" She raised her head from the deck chair and peered at me. "No, dear, that cannot be Wales. It is probably the coast of Ireland." She leaned back and closed her eyes again. Only the chestnut waves and coils on her head looked like Mother. Her face had a pea-green tinge and her usual driving energy was entirely absent.

After eight days at sea we approached the mouth of the St. Lawrence River. Surrounded by massive chunks of ice that concealed the water, the *Royal George* bumped her way through like a stubborn turtle. Icebergs as tall as buildings loomed. At night the foghorn moaned, "No..oo, no..oo" as the ship inched forward behind the searching light.

We landed in Quebec on May 1, 1914. "Why do they have people shut up in those big chicken pens?" Gray asked inside the customs building. Mother, Daisy, Gray and I soon found ourselves inside the heavy wire fencing with the gate closed behind us. The men of the family, Father and Bert, were taken to the desk for questioning.

"Oh, dear, they've found Bert's scar," Mother murmured.

"What is that scar, anyway?" I asked.

"He had a tubercular gland in his neck; it was years ago," Mother said.

"What's a..." Daisy wouldn't let me finish. There was a circle of men around Bert now, all speaking rapid French.

"I wish I knew what they were saying." Mother twisted her handkerchief. "Whatever shall we do if they send us back?"

After all that fuss, Bert was only in the country for a few months. The army didn't care about the scar on his neck.

We boarded the train at Montreal with some bundles of food and Jack, the dog we had brought from England. The ship had provided a cage but now we had nothing to put him in for the baggage car. Mother smuggled him onto the train. When the conductor came into our coach to see the tickets, Mother pushed Jack under the seat and covered him with her long skirt. She handed over the tickets with a generous smile and the conductor moved on.

"It's a good thing Jack kept still," Father said.

"I scratched his head with my foot," Mother said. "That always keeps him quiet." Soon she was chatting with the people sitting across the aisle.

En route to North Bay and Sudbury, Gray and I stared in amazement at mile after mile of dense evergreen. This was the forest we had heard about in England. It was incredibly vast; at the end of the day we were still in the woods. We watched eagerly for lions, tigers and elephants but Canada seemed to be empty of everything except rocks and trees. At one end of the car was a square coal-burning cookstove with a pipe running through the roof. People took turns frying a pan of bacon, stirring a pot of beans and boiling a kettle for tea. It was all very cosy. We left the train at Sudbury for more supplies. A muddy path led to a turnstile and a little shop where we bought bread, butter and eggs. Back on the train Father studied his change. "I think I've been rooked," he said. The conductor yelled, "All aboard!" It was too late to go back for an accounting.

The seats on the train reclined and there was extra sleeping space on wooden platforms secured by day above the windows and let down on chains at night. Gray and I slept there, rocked by the train and lulled by the clickety-clack of the wheels.

We were still in the forest in the morning. "Where are all the houses?" Gray asked Father. In England it was possible to walk from one town to the next.

"We'll come to them in time," Father said. "This is a big country." Later that day we travelled beside Lake Superior. When we get there we'll go for a swim, I thought.

"We'll be at the Lakehead tomorrow," Father said, as though he had read my mind.

The following morning the conductor called through the door, "Next stop, Port Arthur!" We were near the water again. I saw a cluster of boats. And tall gray structures fit for giants to live in.

"Are those Canadian castles?" I asked.

"No," Father said. "They are grain elevators."

"What...?"

"Hush, dear," Mother said. "It's time to get off."

Clarence met us at the station. He was still 5 feet 6 inches tall topped with red hair, still thin as a twig. But he held himself like a soldier and took charge at once. He stopped Mother's flood of questions with a lifted hand, saying, "Wait a bit. We must hustle to catch the streetcar. The trunks will come later by cart." We climbed uphill to Cumberland Street. To our right stood the red brick and gray stone of the Prince Arthur Hotel. Clarence pointed down the block in the same direction to the paler gray mass of the Whalen Building. "It's eight stories high," he said. "They're just finishing it off. I've heard it has marble floors and woodwork of African mahogany."

We left the bustling street for our first ride on a streetcar. Going south on Cumberland it passed two banks, half a dozen hotels and several men's furnishing shops. Most of the buildings were of red brick with large sparkling windows.

"Hmmmm," Father said. "A thriving place. This should do very nicely."

The car turned onto Bay Street and passed a huge lot heaped with lumber. "There's a great deal of construction going on here," Clarence said. "People expect Port Arthur to be a large seaport in a few years. A group of rich Englishmen calling themselves the Canadian Resources and Development Company is improving the land between here and Fort William. We call it Intercity. They talk about transforming wilderness into an area called Interocean Park. Anyway, I've rented a new bungalow there for you."[3] Mother smiled. She leaned forward to see out of the window on Father's side.

She saw open fields and rows of rough shanties squatting on brown grass. "I didn't expect to see slums in Canada," she said.

"That's where the foreigners live," Clarence said. "People

brought in to work on the railway and the breakwater in the harbour."

Our destination was Central Avenue in Intercity. Great black ditches gaped everywhere. "For draining the swamp," Clarence said. A dozen small houses lined each side of the street. There were no gardens or green hedges; we had left spring behind us in Hereford. Our new home was a rented bungalow on bare ground amidst leafless scrub trees and the vast black ditches. Nobody said a word. Clarence had done his best.

A small front verandah softened the box-like house and it wasn't too bad inside. The square living-room was panelled and heated by a wood stove. There was a kitchen, a cubbyhole with a chemical toilet and two bedrooms.

During our time in this house Daisy slept at one end of a single bed, Gray and I at the other. Electric light was a novelty and I played with the switches until Father cuffed me on the ear and sent me outside. Gray and I learned to play cowboys and Indians on vacant lots with the other kids. We dragged home charred wood from a burned-out area nearby. Mother didn't mention our blackened clothes; she needed the fuel. Father and Bert were unable to find steady work.

Gray earned pocket money on weekends caddying at the golf links at the end of Central Avenue. "No, you're too small," he said when I tried to tag along. I complained to Mother.

"Gray is two years older," she said. "Your turn will come." When she had to go out while my brother was caddying she put me on the trolley that ran up and down our street.[4] The conductor was a friendly chap who didn't mind babysitting.

With summer came hordes of mosquitoes bred in the swampy ground that Central Avenue was built on. Long walks around the twin cities provided an escape. One day we stood at the look-out[5] admiring the Sleeping Giant across Thunder Bay. Father's gaze was on Lake Superior. "A fine body of water," he said. "But it's not the sea." He turned away.

Sundays were reserved for services at St. John's Anglican Church in Port Arthur. Soon we had friends and Daisy found employment as a mother's helper with a family called Harper. There were farms at Intercity and Bert was hired to look after a dozen cows. Gray and I helped him. It was a privilege to spend the whole day with this lively brother who was so much older. Mother packed a lunch each morning and we herded the cows to an open field called the Little Prairie. An unfenced railway line ran by the edge of the field, so Bert gave his little brothers the job of keeping strays off the track. This was easy. The challenge lay in driving them to their various homes late in the afternoon. The cows had to be coaxed across May Street, a turmoil of bicycles, horse-drawn wagons and autos. The driver of one of these new-fangled cars, whipping along at ten miles an hour, would tootle his horn now and then. The message to bicycles, wagons, pedestrians and cows was "Out of my way!" At least one cow would bolt each time, lumbering for the safety of the fields, eyes rolling and frayed tail straight up as though electrified.

The First World War ended our cowpunching days and our comradeship with Bert. Great Britain declared war on Germany on August 4, 1914. That same day a poem by Gertrude Cornish Knight appeared in Port Arthur's *Daily News*:

> We are waiting, Mother England
> For thy call across the sea
> When ten thousand shouts will answer
> 'Here I am, send me, send me!'
> When that great voice calls her children
> Ringing clear from shore to shore,
> Then Fair Canada will answer
> Here's a hundred thousand more.

Enlistment offices were flooded with young men who were not only patriotic but unemployed. Bert joined the Princess Patricia's Canadian Light Infantry of Winnipeg – nicknamed the Little Black Devils. Three weeks later the new soldiers took the train east from the Port Arthur depot. Our family clustered around Bert. "Be careful, son." Mother could think of little else to say.

"Don't forget to write every week," Daisy said. She didn't cry, not then. Tears would have embarrassed Bert. He seemed a stranger in his khaki, the cap jaunty on his black head, a lust for adventure burning in his eyes.

The Port Arthur Citizens' Band played "O Canada," "Rule

Britannia" and "Auld Lang Syne." When the train pulled away to the notes of "God Save the King," men took off their hats and the crowd sang along with the band.

The nationwide recession of 1913 had reached the Lakehead the winter before we arrived. Indeed, only a few days before war was declared the *Daily News* had run an article recommending a movement back to the land as a solution. Clarence met a man named Taffy Jones who had taken up a homestead in Dinorwic, about 200 miles west of the Lakehead on the CPR line. "It only costs a dollar for 160 acres and you can live real cheap," Taffy said. "Free firewood, lots of fish and game, it's a fine life." Clarence filed at once but we didn't move until December. Daisy stayed behind. She was earning room and board and $5 a month at the Harpers.

2

RABBITS AND PLUM PUDDING

he train chugged away and left us in the wilderness. A couple of mutts rolled on the station platform, snarling, tearing at matted coats with yellow teeth. An anguished yelp escaped as the fangs of one of them drew blood. Otherwise all was still. The station master had gone to unload our baggage and we were silent at Dinorwic station as we stared up the hill at four unpainted frame buildings and a tiny white church at the top. I wondered if it had oak pews and stained glass windows like St. John's in Port Arthur. The seven months at the Lakehead seemed like a dream already; or maybe this was the dream, the five of us standing in an empty, blinding whiteness, hemmed in by dark evergreens on one side and the frozen, snow-piled lake on the other side behind the railway tracks.

Single file we slogged up the hill, our city boots slipping on the hard-packed snow on the trail. Clarence, who had come to Dinorwic before us, was in the lead. Halfway up he stopped and pointed to a ramshackle house propped by snowbanks that nudged the bare windows. A narrow path slashed through white dunes to the weathered door.

"This is it, folks," he said. "I cleared the walk just before the train came in. Sorry I didn't have time to get the heater going."

Father stared at the house in silence. Mother said, "Whoever had this certainly didn't look after it."

"Nobody's lived here since the Gold Rock mines⁶ closed three years ago," Clarence said. "It was the best I could do now since we can't build on the homestead in December."

"Let's go in and make a fire," Mother said. Inside, light

glinted between shrunken boards. Later we discovered that the chinking had dried and fallen away from the logs these boards concealed. Now everyone stared at the cold heater in the centre of the frigid room and the crumbling pieces of bark on the cracked linoleum.

Numb toes stirred my longing for the fireplaces of Hereford. The clean smell of fresh-cut wood in the basket; the softness of the carpet as I sank to my knees to watch the fire. The crackle of flames as they licked the grate.

"Eric! Stop dreaming and help your brother bring in some wood." Mother spoke with unusual sharpness and I scuttled to the back door with Gray. It groaned and shuddered when we pushed with all our might but the white coverlet on the other side came halfway up the door.

"Someone will have to clear a path to the back," Clarence said. He glanced at the mottled legs exposed by the short British pants Gray and I wore, then went out and plucked a shovel from the drift beside the front walk.

"Please, God, send us some wood," I prayed silently. Clarence was short and skinny. It would take him forever to beat his way to the back of the house. And who said there was fuel out there anyway? Mother and Father always told us, "Ask and ye shall receive," so I asked once more, "Please God, send us some wood."

A sound intruded on my thoughts — a chink, chink, chink similar to the rattle of a tambourine. It came from the direction of the hill. Gray and I dashed outside. A man stood beside a toboggan piled with firewood cut to stove length. His jacket was checked red and black, his face the colour of tobacco. Our sister Daisy's words, spoken as we stood at the rail when our steamer left Southhampton, came to mind: "My teacher says that Canada is full of savages." Was this person a savage? I opened my mouth to ask him just as he said, "I'm Jim Isbester. Brought you folks some wood to start off with. We live a bit further up the hill." He bent to stack wood on his left arm, then strolled in silent moccasins to the open door where Mother and Father waited with astonished smiles.

Gray and I moved a little closer to the sleigh dogs who sat patiently on their haunches. Red and blue pompons and round bells in matching colours adorned their leather collars. We learned later that Mr. Isbester was a typical trapper. Most were half-breeds. All took pride in decorating their dog teams.

When the firewood was inside the house our good neighbour knelt on the toboggan, said "Mush!" and the dogs careened down the hill, red and blue ribbons streaming from their harness.

"Boys," Clarence said from behind us, "Take the washtub from the house and get some water. Go down the hill and across the track to the lake. The path is open right to the water hole in the ice. There's a sack full of straw in the hole to keep it from freezing over. Be sure to replace it after you fill the tub."

In the house, Mother and Father stood close to the heater, rubbing their hands. They still wore coats and hats. "It's warming up nicely," Mother said with a smile. "And Clarence has gone to see about the furniture." She was referring to a collection of furniture we had bought at the Lakehead. It was now sitting on the station platform with our trunks. Clarence and another man would carry everything to the house piece by piece.

The galvanized washtub hung on a two-inch spike next to an enamel basin and a torn towel so filthy that the original colour was blotted out. We took the tub out to the crest of the hill, jumped inside and shoved off. It was too wide for the trail so we gave up and took turns kicking it the rest of the way down.

Near the edge of the water hole we found a dipper – an empty can, labelled "coal oil," with wire handles. We took turns filling our tub and Gray led the way home, holding his side of the container with a hand behind his back. Our feet slipped on the trail and water sloshed on my boots. The going was easier on the new path to the back of the house where the lean-to kitchen sagged away from the main building. "Watch out!" I yelled as my foot caught on the doorsill. I crashed into Gray, his shoes skidded on the linoleum and water flooded the floor. It was freezing by the time we scrambled to our feet.

Although the cookstove was in the lean-to we had to close off the room for the winter. The ice on the floor would not yield to a fire in the stove because the gap where the kitchen extension pulled away admitted a merciless cold that seized the room until spring thaw. We didn't need an icebox. The freezing kitchen preserved the moosemeat Jim gave us that winter and the rabbits he taught us to snare. He was the agent of our survival in those first bleak months in the bush but he remained Mr. Isbester to all of us. It was not customary for British people to call those outside the family by their first names. After we moved to the homestead later on one of our neighbours, Taffy Jones, became an exception to this rule. Calling this man Mr. would have been like putting a silk topper on a scarecrow. He had no use for dignity or respect. He answered to Taffy, a name derived from an old rhyme that English children used to chant:

> Taffy was a Welshman
> Taffy was a thief
> Taffy came to our house
> And stole a leg of beef.

This neighbour of ours was not a thief. His nationality was enough to earn him the nickname. Taffy's nationality may also have made Dinorwic seem an attractive place to live, since there was a village of the same name in Wales.

Mr. Isbester had a small shack on Little Sandy Lake, four or five miles from the village. He took Gray and me there for ice-fishing. When we stayed overnight he made bannock in a frying pan on the tin stove. Flat, crisp and brown, it had a slightly sour tang. We loved it.

At the Lakehead we had carried on our old custom of eating four or five meals a day which included the English high tea at four o'clock and the later supper at eight. In Dinorwic we tightened our belts and settled for three meals a day and those were quite plain. Fish and moosemeat varied the usual fare, which was fried, stewed or baked rabbit. For a treat Mother made plum duff, also called rolypoly – dough rolled and spread with jam, then rolled again into a linen cloth and boiled. The jammy smell hung sweet and heavy in the warm air near the stove. When Mother sliced it, fresh from the pot, Gray and I burned our tongues on rich sticky bits snatched from the cutting-board.

We missed the treacle pudding she used to make in Hereford. All we could buy in Dinorwic was corn syrup – in our opinion a poor substitute for Lyle's Golden Treacle, which came in a green can with a lion on the label and a hovering cloud of bees. Treacle was thicker than syrup; it rolled slowly over the tongue and lingered on the roof of the mouth. Pancakes were never the same without it.

But the favourite treat in Hereford had been Mother's Christmas puddings, which she made in November and stored for a year. This December of 1914 Gray and I lay on our cots and talked ourselves to sleep. "I suppose we won't have turkey this year," Gray said. "Mr. Wimble will give ours to someone else." Every year in Hereford a friend of Mother's had delivered a fat bird to our door on Christmas Eve.

"And no pudding," I said. "It's too late for Mother to make them now. Oh! We won't have one next year, either!"

Gray and I had always helped with the puddings, stoning the big black raisins, chopping the suet (smooth and soapy on our fingers), cutting the sticky green and yellow peel. All of it went into the huge white, gold-rimmed basin that usually rested with its fluted pitcher on the commode in our parents' bedroom. Each member of the family stirred the pudding once for luck. Then mother divided it into smaller bowls, covered them with white cloths securely tied with string, and steamed them for eight hours in a large pot used on ordinary days for boiling clothes in the scullery. I could smell the pudding now, spicy and tantalizing.

"I liked going with Father to buy the Yule log," Gray said, "and dragging it home with a rope."

"And roasting chestnuts in the embers," I said. "And the small presents in the bran tub on Boxing Day. Remember how Daisy used to sneeze?"

We reviewed Christmas past like old men living on memories. The holiday season had always been the same since Gray and I were born. Now our lives had been turned topsy-turvy. We were chessmen, swept from the board by a witch's broom. Bert was at war, Daisy at the Lakehead, and our oldest sister, Win, still in Hereford. Just Clarence, Gray, myself and our parents would celebrate the holy day in the shack we now called home. And the proof of poverty was all around us.

In Hereford the warning signs had passed unnoticed by two small boys growing up in a rambling home surrounded by walled gardens and ancient hills. Here, dense dark bush loomed beyond fields and banks and hummocks of snow. There was no flower-bright paper on the walls of the house, just the heavy black building variety nailed on by Clarence and Father in an attempt to stem the relentless cold. An icy floor slapped our bare feet in the mornings. Worst of all, we saw no bustle of holiday preparation. "It's Christmas all the same," Mother said. "Don't mope about, you'll upset your father."

On the morning of December 25 I nearly fell down the rickety stairs. An enormous evergreen soared to the ceiling. Bows of red wool draped the branches, tufts of white rabbit fur clung to them like snow. A large parcel waited, wrapped in brown paper dotted with Christmas seals. We had never had a tree in England; they were too expensive.

Morning prayer was much too long on this day. Now and then I lifted my head to peek at the parcel. What could it be? It wasn't big enough to be a sled. Not a lumpy package, it was something in a box.

In the Old Country we had gone to church with Father on Christmas morning while Mother cooked mid-day dinner. The presents piled on the drawing-room table were not touched until after the meal. Father disappeared after the plum pudding "to take a nap." Soon afterward the brass knocker on the front door clacked twice and there stood Father Christmas dressed in red with a white beard brushing his chest. He kissed Mother under the mistletoe. One year he even kissed our next-door neighbour. Then he passed around our presents.

We learned who Father Christmas really was when we saw the beard and the suit while Mother was turning out the house in Hereford for the auction sale. They were gone, the suit and the beard, gone with so many other things that had coloured the first eight years of my life.

There were no stockings to rummage in this year, and after morning prayer Mother said we could open the parcel right away. The paper ripped easily from the croquinole set Clarence had bought with money he earned cutting wood. This was a gift for the whole family and we played with it daily for the rest of that winter and for many winters to come. That Christmas morning Mother said, "Go ahead, have a game while I make the stuffing for the rabbit."

We were into our third round of play when Gray and I sniffed and jumped from our chairs, upsetting the game board. "It's pudding!" I said. "Plum pudding!" Nothing else on earth gave off such a rich fruity smell. Mother chuckled. "I stowed two of them in my trunk," she said. "What's Christmas dinner without pudding?"

She set the table with a linen cloth, darned in the middle but gleaming white, and the Blue Willow china. We hadn't left *everything* behind.

The Ancestor watched from his gilded frame with the solemn gaze that had presided over all our dinners in the house in Hereford. The oil portrait was nearly life-size, the background dead black. His hair was russet, his face stolid, but the icy blue eyes seemed to follow you as you moved about the room. Although his name had been forgotten his influence still prevailed. Generations of Rhinds had minded their manners under that forbidding stare. His paint had never been restored and deep cracks marred the dignity of his pose. I wondered how he liked his new home. Mother raised her head from saying grace and met the eyes of the Ancestor. Her chin quivered.

3

DESPERATE WINTER

The parcel from Daisy arrived a few days later. She had taken her month's pay to the five-and-dime store and selected gifts for all of us except Father. For him she had knitted a lumpy purple scarf which he wore everywhere for several winters.

Mother and Father worried about Daisy. She wanted to support herself, to ease the burden on our parents, but she had not accepted the move from England. "Dead cats and tin cans," she had said when we took a walk in Intercity the previous spring. "In Hereford we'd be looking for the first primrose now." It was true; here the melting snow revealed only squalor.

Now snow was falling again. If Mother longed for the roses of England that held their blooms into December, she never said so. In Dinorwic this winter of 1914-1915 she was making a new home. She pulled the tapestry table-cover from her trunk and chopped it into curtains for the two small windows and cushions for the folding cot that served as a couch. The cushions were plumped with rabbit fur. Flour sacks became dish-towels, aprons and underwear. Mother did all this by hand. She didn't have a sewing machine until years later.

Sewing was done in the daytime. Mother and Father went to bed early to save coal oil. They slept so close to the stove that one night a corner of their blanket smouldered. They woke in time to douse it and avoid disaster. The rest of us climbed the quivering staircase each night to the one upstairs room.

It was warmer there and I fell into dreams that persisted after eight months in Canada. Awake, I never thought of the crossing;

asleep, I could not escape it. My stomach churned and I ran for the rail. Daisy said, "A future for the boys, what about me?" Huge beasts plunged in the ocean, their spray making rainbows in the sunshine. "Mother, come and see the whales!" She raised her head from the deck chair. Her eyes were raisins, her face a white pudding.

I woke in time to see Father crack icicles from his moustache and Mother sit up in bed, her long hair loose on her shoulders. Back in Hereford, I used to watch her dress it in the morning. Her hair crackled and clung to the ivory-backed brush when she lifted it. Her fingers raced, crimping waves above her forehead, braiding little coils to perch over close-set ears. Then she was ready to direct our lives for another day.

Here in Dinorwic she huddled inside an afghan while her fingers in slow motion made a knot at the back of her head. Often her face had a blurred and blotchy look but when Father had the stove roaring she became her old brisk and busy self.

The walls of the heater glowed red on washday. Gray and I made countless trips to the lake. We kept a barrel in the house and dumped snow into it daily. However, a pail of snow melted to a mere puddle of water. Mother rubbed cottons on the washboard and boiled them on the stove. Father took the steaming laundry from the wash-boiler with a broom handle and they were pegged to the line outside to whiten in the frost. Garments frozen to the clothes-line sometimes ripped when pried loose, so eventually Mother strung lines in the house and we dodged dripping shirts and camisoles and icy patches on the floor.

When the laundry was nearly dry Mother tackled it again with three-pound irons heated on the stove. If the flick of a wet finger made the iron hiss it was ready for work. Mother's special irons for sleeves, tucks and flounces had been sacrificed to the auction sale. As time passed her pleated shirtwaists and ruffled blouses were replaced by plain cotton house-dresses often sewn from the same kind of sacks she used for tea-towels.

She saved bath water and scrubbed the floor with it. She filled lamps, trimmed wicks, polished the glass chimneys. If Mother missed the running water, gaslight and rugs of her old home she never said so. "Don't worry your father" was a household rule. However, she didn't hesitate to prod him into action when necessary. She needed everyone's help that first desperate winter.

Mother left the house to attend church services twice a month. Occasionally, in a thin black coat and a velvet hat she would go the other way to the Hudson's Bay store. She had to remind herself that there was life beyond the shabby house and the snow that threatened to bury us all.

When the mail train whistled one of us always hurried to the store where the manager was also the postmaster. Sometimes this train went right through Dinorwic. Close to the track stood a post with two hinged pieces called mail arms. These had rings for attaching outgoing bags. A lever swung out from the door of the train to catch the bag on the fly. Incoming mail was simply kicked off the train. For weeks we heard nothing of Bert, who was somewhere on the front lines in France.

4

MONKEY NUTS

Daisy wrote once a week, still lonely for the family. She had joined the choir of St. Luke's Anglican Church in Fort William. On Saturdays she took six-year-old Lillian Harper to the Orpheum Theatre where they enjoyed silent movies and vaudeville shows. She had learned to skate. But her anxiety about Bert was growing. Every day she scanned the casualty lists posted outside the newspaper office in Port Arthur. Although Mother knew that bad news would come first by telegram, she tore open Daisy's letters in great haste. Then she bustled about more than ever to clear a mental picture of the casualty lists from her mind.

That winter mother cut up an old coat and made knickers for Gray and me, pants that covered the knees. She knitted woolen socks to match and lined moosehide moccasins with rabbit fur. People said that our English blood, thicker than the Canadian variety, would protect us that first winter. Mother wasn't taking any chances.

We played on the hill with Kathleen Quinn, whose parents ran the hotel. She was nine, just between Gray and me in age, blonde, saucy and daring. She taught us how to belly-flop onto her toboggan and steer it down the hill. At the bottom, trains ran through a fenced cut ten feet deep. Kathleen was soon bored with merely sliding as far as the fence. "Tie up those wires, Gray," she said. "Let's see if we can make it across the track." She *would* ask Gray, I thought, just because he was older.

"I'll do it," I said, so he and I both dashed down the hill and raised the wire fence with a piece of rope. Then we all swooped through the cut and hit the nearest rail with a jolt that knocked us from the toboggan. Kathleen's dress flew up and exposed her flannel bloomers. Gray and I jumped up and turned our backs. Kathleen laughed as she brushed off the snow. "You boys are pretty green," she said. "Never seen bloomers before?" We hadn't, except on the clothes-line. Here was a mystery that begged to be solved but Kathleen, our first and only female playmate, revealed no more than her bloomers. Every time she called us green we felt the weight of our ignorance.

There was so much to learn. Larry Williams, manager of the Hudson's Bay store, lived on our hill. One day I ran to his store with a penny inside my mitten. Stacks of groceries filled one side of the room, dry goods and hardware the other. Long counters ran in front of both sections. "Come on fellows, MOVE!" the manager said to the rows of Ojibway men who sat on the counters like crows on a fence. Nobody budged. "Oh well," he said, "what can I do for you, sonny?"

I held out my penny and asked for the treat I had shared so often with the organ-grinder's pet back home. "I'll have one cent's worth of monkey nuts, please."

Dinorwic station, with the Hudson's Bay Company store and manager's house on the right.

"What's that?" Mr. Williams asked. I thought he must be deaf.

"A penny's worth of those *monkey nuts!*"

"We don't sell monkey's nuts." The Indians on the counters snickered. Eight years of training in politeness vanished. "You people are all crazy!" I shouted. "There's a whole keg of monkey nuts RIGHT HERE!" I shoved the container with my foot.

"*We* call them peanuts," Mr. Williams said, grinning.

Soon after this episode Clarence was hired as a clerk in the store. He went to live in the manager's house and began to pay off our bill for coal oil, sugar, tea, flour and footwear. Clarence became a fur buyer and we realized that snaring rabbits was small-time stuff. The money was in other furs. Our brother gave us a couple of traps. The first time we checked them there was a weasel in mine, still alive and furious. It glared with murderous eyes and thrashed wildly as we approached the trap.

"Look at those teeth!" I said. "Let's get out of here."

"Don't be a sissy," Gray said. "Bash him over the head." Clutching a stout piece of wood I struck at the weasel's head and missed as he snapped at my fingers.

"You do it, you're bigger," I said.

"Not me, it's your trap!"

The club found its mark on my next try but the animal was only dazed. It lunged for my hand again when I touched the trap. The weasel has a skull like a rock. By the time this one lay dead I was sweating. And we had no idea what to do next.

A half-breed friend of ours, Jim Williams, had shown us how to set the traps so we went to him for a lesson in skinning. He was just about to skin a weasel of his own.

"Sure," he said. "It's easy, just watch." He cut down the inside of the back legs and around the feet, pulled the legs out and cut across the tail.

"Have to be careful here," he said as he gently pulled out the long thin tailbone. "That black tip on the end of the tail is where the money is. That's what they put on the King's robe." Jim eased the fur up, cut off the feet and pulled the fur over the head like a mother peeling a sweater from a child.

"O.K. Eric, now you do yours." I took the knife and made the first cut.

"You dummy," Gray said. "Look at the blood! You cut too deep!"

"I *did* not," I said. "I cut my blasted finger!"

Jim grinned. "Dead weasels don't bleed," he said. "Here, Gray, you do it, and be careful, scrape with the dull edge of the knife and just bring it up slow. That's all there is to it. Now bring me a board off that apple box and I'll show you how to make a stretcher."

After that day we were able to do the job ourselves. A weasel skin was worth 75 cents to $1.25. A mink pelt earned $5, enough for a week's groceries, but trapping a mink was a rare event for us. The price of muskrat hovered somewhere between those figures. Sometimes Mother fried muskrat legs for dinner. They were tender and had only a slight taste of the wild.

We didn't earn much money with our traps but Father treated each sum as a valuable contribution. The money went into the cash box. He entered the amount in his ledger with the name of the one who had earned it. This account book was consulted whenever Gray and I wanted something from Eaton's catalogue; Father's ledger always had the last word.

Meanwhile the school was open again. Gray and I completed the roster of ten pupils required for the hiring of a teacher. We waited uneasily for the first day of school. The teacher we had had at Intercity was a young girl who had no control of the class. What if we drew someone like the headmaster of the Blue Coat School in Hereford?

As it turned out, our first teacher in Dinorwic was Miss McGuire, a frail middle-aged lady with heart disease who could not climb the hill each day. She slept on a cot in the one-room school and cooked on the heater.

The ten pupils were at various levels of learning. For those who didn't know their ABC's, the story of the Little Red Hen was as unreadable as it was for us, caught up in Father's nightly rendition of *Great Expectations*.

Miss McGuire's long serge skirt swept the aisle as she gave us individual attention. Once Jim Williams, the half-breed boy who had taught us how to skin and stretch furs, hacked and hacked in school with a continuous rasping bark. Our teacher boiled some

Gray (left) and Eric as young trappers.

water, then added honey and lemon extract. "Try this, Jim," she said. He swallowed several doses with relish. In the morning Gray and I entered the classroom coughing. Esther Lawrence was the next victim, then her brothers, followed by the rest of the class. The teacher surveyed us, trying not to smile, then she mixed her concoction and boiled it. When the pot was empty everyone was cured and we got back to work. We worked for her after school too, keeping track of those who filled the wood box and carried the water so that everyone had their turn.

Since Gray and I lived just downhill from the school we were usually the first pupils to arrive. With the March wind at our backs we went up the hill one morning.

"Look at the stovepipe. There's no smoke!" Gray said. He hurried to open the door and I paused to grab an armful of wood. Gray hadn't closed the door and he was standing in the middle of the room. Miss McGuire lay on her narrow cot. Her hair had escaped its bun and straggled around her thin white face. One skinny arm was flung over her head. The sleeve of her nightgown was torn.

Words darted through my mind: a rag, a bone and a hank of hair. My arms went limp and the wood crashed to the floor. Miss McGuire didn't move.

"Why do people die, Father?" I asked.

"Because God calls them home. Don't grieve, son. Miss McGuire has gone to a better place." I supposed that there was a terrible shortage of teachers in heaven but surely God could have found one somewhere else.

The school was closed again and Father became our tutor. He led us through the French Revolution and the nineteenth-century workhouse. I've always thought he invented the cliff-hanger for he stopped each tale at a place that made us eager for the next episode. His math lessons, however, were of no practical value since he used an old text of sums set in pounds, shillings and pence. He knew the Canadian money system; perhaps he thought we would return to England one day. Soon Daisy, who had been a pupil-teacher in Hereford, came home and took over our education until another teacher came to Dinorwic.

We had no newspaper in those early years. War news came to the village via the station agent, Mr. McFarlane, who picked it up in condensed form over the wire. In April 1915 we heard of the Battle of Ypres and the poison gas used by the Germans.

"I do hope Bert wasn't there!" Mother said.

"All we can do is pray, Lizzie," Father said.

We had prayed for Bert ever since he left home but now he was never out of our thoughts. Soon the telegram came. Bert was missing in action.

"He can't be dead, not Bert, he can't..." Daisy said this often, as though her faith could spirit Bert away from the gas rolling in thick yellow clouds over Canadian soldiers and set him down in some safe spot in Europe.

Bert and Win in England at the beginning of the First World War.

5

THE MEN'S ROOM

Quinn's Hotel in Dinorwic, a big frame house with many upstairs bedrooms, had prospered in years past when the Grand Trunk Pacific Railway[7] was under construction. Heavy supplies such as tools and blasting powder came to Dinorwic on the CPR and were hauled north in winter. Men hired to work on the Grand Trunk stayed at the hotel en route. There were also patrons from the glory days of the Gold Rock mines to the south. During our years in Dinorwic, people on their way to pulpwood camps formed the bulk of the hotel's clients.

Quinn's Hotel, Dinorwic.

Occasionally a travelling salesman jumped from the bottom step of the eastbound passenger train and strode to the baggage car to oversee the unloading of his trunk. All "trunk men" looked alike to me. They stuck out their chins and walked importantly but their cheeks were hollow. The veins on their hands looked like worms and the pants of their striped suits were shiny at the seams and the creases. Everything inside their battered trunks was spanking new: crisp cotton yard goods, bright buttons, shiny ribbons, lace collars, felt boots, fur hats, toys, books, pocket watches. I loved to be in the Hudson's Bay store when a trunk man slowly pulled out each sample item and slapped it on the counter with a flourish. He was the next best thing to a magician.

Indians bringing in furs from their traplines also stayed at Quinn's Hotel until the Hudson's Bay Company built Indian House, which served as accommodation right beside the store.

Mr. Quinn was Irish. He radiated good fellowship and whisky fumes. He and I clicked instantly. He allowed me to do chores around the hotel and often invited me to supper. I peeled potatoes

Quinn's party, 1916. Lizzie Rhind kneels on the left beside Mrs. Isbester.
Daisy is in front of her beside Rosie Jones, Taffy's daughter.
The girl with the bow in her hair is Kathleen Quinn.

for Mrs. Quinn, a large resigned lady whom I can still picture sweating beside the huge camp stove covered in big bubbling pots. The family, hired help and hotel guests ate together at the great table in the dining-room. One evening Bill Milroy, an employee, dashed from the room to get his rifle. Firing from the open window, he dropped a bull moose standing at the edge of the clearing. Everyone in Dinorwic had fresh meat that week.

The Men's Room was the most fascinating spot in the hotel. It was not a beer parlour but a meeting place with a wood stove, a spitoon and a circle of kitchen chairs where men sat to discuss topics of interest. Too young to join the group, I used the keyhole or the crack behind the door when it was left ajar.

One day a Negro appeared as a guest of the hotel. With his dignified bearing, good manners and American accent, he may have been a porter on a Pullman car. The only odd thing about his appearance was an ugly facial scar. He took a seat in the Men's Room and everyone said hello.

Bill Milroy asked, "What's your name?"

"Frank," the man answered, looking quickly around the room. "Frank...Hazelwood." All eyes turned to the stove where the brand name Hazelwood stood out in letters three inches high. Well, a man had a right to his secrets. Frank Hazelwood he remained until he shot himself years later after a long slide into madness.

Hazelwood acquired a couple of cabins in the bush to the north of us, which made him the only person living between Dinorwic and Sioux Lookout. The following year, wealthy Americans came to stay with him for the hunting season. Mr. Hazelwood was a jolly person at this time. He played the banjo and sang "Oh Susannah" and other ballads of the day when he came to visit.

"Come and spend the weekend at my place," he often said to Gray and me. All our pleading was in vain. Mother would not allow her sons to go nine miles back in the bush with someone who had a secret past and a ragged scar on his cheek.

But visitors, including Frank Hazelwood, were always welcome at our house. Mother and Father couldn't hide their excitement when a trunk man or a minister, anyone from the outside world, dropped in. Only one of our chairs had arms.

When company was expected Gray and I moved the "visitor's chair" an inch at a time until it stood directly under a hole in our bedroom floor. We took a piece of fine thread upstairs at bedtime and tied it to a dead spider or a pillow feather. This was dropped through the hole in front of the guest's face and instantly yanked back up. Our parents were so starved for conversation that it was months before they noticed that everyone who came had the strange habit of brushing the tip of his nose.

Frank Hazelwood's visits to our house soon came to an end. He looked at Daisy too often when he played love songs on the banjo. One night he slipped her a note. My best efforts could not uncover the content of that note, and I didn't see Frank again except at the store or, later on when I drove a team of horses, at his place in the bush. Frank was forty years old while Daisy was still in her teens. He had a mysterious, possibly criminal, past. And he was coloured. Frank had presumed too much.

In March 1916 we heard at last from Bert. The postcard came from a prison camp in Munster, Germany. But he was alive! The family rejoiced and offered prayers of thanksgiving.

That same year the Reverend Mr. Bruce, an Anglican minister, lived in Dinorwic. He did some trapping and sometimes

> Dear Daisy
>
> Just a few line to let you know that I am OK; hopeing you, & all home are the same. I am so glade you are nearer home as you will be able to pop home pretty often, Well Old Girl just get a hurry & send me some more snapshot I think the one's you sent just OK. must stop now lots of love.

held services in Dinorwic's Anglican church, St. George's which did not have a regular minister at the time. He came to our house often and one day he said to Daisy, "Why don't you learn the Morse code? With so many men at war there must be openings for women in the field."

My sister liked the idea and sent for a "dummy key" and a battery for power. She struggled with the dots and dashes for weeks. "It's no use," she said at last. "I'll have to go to school." Through friends at the Lakehead she found a position as housekeeper to fund her attendance at business college in Fort William, where she studied Morse and typing at night. She had finally made a commitment to her new country.

6

ON WITH THE DANCE

he Indian Reserve[8] was about five miles away across Dinorwic Lake. On a clear night the throbbing of the drums carried to the village. Each fall the Indians came to town to get supplies for their trap lines. They boiled wild rice in a pot suspended over a fire in the centre of a triangle of poles. Hudson's Bay wool shirts mingled with buckskin. All the men wore large black felt hats. For celebrations they decked themselves in traditional dress.

The first powwow dance I saw was held behind the store in honour of a Hudson's Bay Company anniversary. The villagers watched from the shadows near the fire. Ojibway men, women and children joined hands and shuffled in a circle. The drumbeat quickened, the drummers yelled "Ay-ay-ay" and the young braves took over the dance. Stripped to the waist, they wore two pieces of cloth tied to conceal their lower bodies. Plumes circled their head and fluttered down their backs to the breech cloths. Deerhide lavished with eagle and owl feathers and porcupine quills wrapped them from knee to ankle. More feathers dripped from wrist bracelets. Sweat ran down tawny chests as they leaped higher and higher, twisting their bodies in movements improvised by each one. As a change of pace they stamped around the circle echoing the "Ay-ay-ay" of the drummers.

When one group tired another knew the exact moment to slip into its place. A burning log collapsed with a WHOOSH! My feet kept time to the boom-boom-boom of the drums. I poked Gray with my elbow. "Say! Don't you wish you were an Indian?"

"Don't be stupid," he said, "who wants to jump about half naked and howling like an idiot?"

By the time I was a teenager the powwow had become a humdrum affair. Once I spent a sleepless night on the reserve longing for the peace and quiet of my own bed. It happened this way. Bill Atkins was chief clerk at the Hudson's Bay store in Dinorwic, and when they needed extra help he called on me. One summer Bill took me to the reserve at treaty time. The government paid the chief $25 and each band member $5. The Indians valued this money more than the large amounts they were getting for furs and they used it for a long night of celebration. In the Hudson's Bay tent we set out candy, cigarettes and canned fruit.

The treaty ceremony came first. Dignitaries approached the reserve in boats: the Indian agent, the paymaster, an Anglican minister who might be needed for a marriage or a baptism, a couple of Mounties in scarlet coats. The natives stood in a straight and solemn line on the shore. As the treaty party approached they raised their rifles and fired a welcoming volley at an angle across the lake. The chief wore a naval jacket adorned with medals; one had the image of Queen Victoria, another was a Hudson's Bay Company medal presented to him on that anniversary when I had been so thrilled by the powwow.

When the official party left, the Indians lined up once more and sent them off with another round of gunfire. Then the bootleggers came out of the bush and the dance began.

There was no hope of sleep for Bill and me with the boom-boom-boom, the ay-ay-ay and the customers constantly streaming into the tent. All our stock was gone by morning. We pulled away in our little motor boat from a scene littered with empty bottles and cans, bodies prone on the ground, and a few die-hards still bounding about as though they would never run down.

In the fall the Hudson's Bay Company grubstaked the Ojibway with food, traps, tobacco and other supplies for the trap lines. Later they paid off the debts with weasel, mink, beaver, fox, marten, fisher, bobcat and wolf. When they returned to the trap lines they owed the company for another grubstake.

The arrangement between the company and the natives suited both parties. Occasionally an itinerant fur buyer quietly dropped off the train and tempted the Indians with ready cash.

The store manager was resigned to losing a few furs in this way. It made no difference to the supremacy of the great Hudson's Bay Company.

Periodically the clerks sorted the wealth of furs and baled them for shipping in a canvas called Russian Sheeting. When I saw the furs piled in the long dim room – the dark and glossy mink, the weasel in its winter white, and all the others soft and gleaming in the lamp light – I felt as a boy might who stood in a bank vault surrounded by unimaginable riches.

7

CREEKSIDE

By late March 1916 the pile of wood ashes in the back yard was higher than the sinking snow. Mother knew that our hill would soon be slimy with mud; she sat with the Eaton's catalogue on her knee comparing the price of rubbers with the amount of money in the cash box. Then Clarence came in with news that drove the problem from her mind.

"We'll build on the homestead this spring," he said. "I've bought an old house from the Hudson's Bay Company. They had no use for it and sold it for a pittance. We'll tear it down and use the materials for our place."

McKenzie Creek flowed by our property. "Let's build near the water and call the place Creekside," Mother said. "And I can have a flower garden! Zinnias, sweet peas, do you think a rose garden would survive the winter?"

"First we have to get the house built," Clarence said. "We'll start on the old building this weekend."

Board by board it came down. Our brother gave Gray and me the job of straightening each bent nail pried from the wood. Stanley Korzinski, the pumphouse man,[9] accepted the task of building a house on our homestead a mile east of the railroad station. All of us learned to pound nails and saw boards. That summer we moved into the unfinished place. There were no screens on doors or windows. We burned smudge pots before bedtime, then dove under the mosquito nets Mother made to drape over the beds. One night a bat got into the house. Another time there was a garter snake curled up in my bed. "Don't open that window too wide," I said to Gray one stifling August night, "or we'll have wolves in here next."

The house was divided into a combination kitchen and living-room and two bedrooms. Outside were acres of trees that Gray and I would have to clear if our family was ever to receive an affidavit naming the Rhinds owners of the property. Homesteads were granted to induce people to turn large tracts of bush into farm land. Fifteen acres had to be under cultivation before a settler could apply for a patent.

Creekside, the Rhind homestead at Dinorwic, c. 1925.

The first morning in our new home, Gray and I, aged ten and twelve, went out with our axes. We could see the creek in front of the house and the railroad tracks on the right-hand side. Some clearing had been done to make space for building the house. To the left and rear of the building the small open spaces dissolved into solid walls of evergreen and poplar. Neither of us admitted how hopeless our task appeared. We marched up to the largest spruce on the edge of the clearing and took turns whacking it as hard as we could. When it fell with a splintering crash we looked at the stump still firmly rooted in the earth.

"How do we get rid of that?" I asked Gray.

"Let's go ask someone at the Lawrence place. They'll know, they've been here for years." We set off across the tracks to the trail that led eastward to the Lawrence homestead. Although we had met some of the children in school this was our first visit to their house.

"There it is," Gray said as we reached open ground. The door of the unpeeled log building was propped open with a rusty spade. A black-and-white calf wandered across the yard and into the house. A tall woman with wild pepper and salt hair said, "Come in boys, yer just in time for breakfast." The one room was partitioned with curtains nailed to the ceiling. At one end, tousled heads peeked from the folds like baby birds from a nest.

"Esther, Thomas, Peter, Ruth, Mary, git out here," Mrs. Lawrence bawled. "They're named from the Bible," she told us. That was odd – we had never seen a Lawrence in church.

She removed dirty plates from the table and poured glasses of milk, flicking something black from one with the tip of a spoon. "Have a seat," she said, pointing to the blocks of wood placed around the table. The calf stuck his head between us and knocked over the milk pitcher. A fat black fly rose from the sugar bowl and settled on the calf's tail. Gray and I stood up.

"We can't stay, thank you," I said. "We came to ask how to get rid of stumps."

"Well, my oldest sons work on the track, they're gone already, and Mr. Lawrence he's at Osaquan, don't get home much. But Sam can help you, he's out back splitting wood."

A skinny boy with jet black hair looked down at us, grinning. "You kids are clearing that homestead?"

"Yes, we started this morning. If you'd just tell us about the stumps..."

"Stumping powder. Blow 'em the hell out of the ground."

"We don't have any," Gray said.

"Then you gotta dig 'em out. And chop the roots off and pry them out with long poles. First off you cut down saplings and peel them to make the poles."

We thanked him and went home. By the end of the day we had six trees cut and four stumps dug out. Sore and exhausted, we went to bed right after supper. Gradually we got used to the work and to the realization that we would never get fifteen acres cleared. Sometimes we had other things to do, such as swimming in the deep cool water under the shadow of the railway bridge.

Soon after we moved to Creekside, Daisy came home to spend time with the station agent, Mr. Shapland. He took her in to observe and to practise on a spare key. Sending the Morse code was as individual as handwriting; some people had a "good fist" and others were hard to read. Daisy often went back to the station at night and took me with her. The scent of sweeping compound lingered beyond the door. The secret chatter of the key, the chains that governed the signals, the view of moonlit rail from the bay window – all these were tokens of the wide world far from this station in the bush. I was proud of my sister's determination to be a telegraph operator.

She studied the rule book daily and the family quizzed her until she was letter perfect. Daisy passed the test in Kenora and became night operator in Dinorwic in 1917 just as the fall grain rush began. Mrs. Johnson, wife of the new Hudson's Bay manager, was scandalized. "Railroading!" she cried. "That's no job for a lady!" Daisy laughed. She was not cut out to be a lady. She spoke of hot boxes and clearances and shunting. She worked from seven at night until seven in the morning.

During the fall, grain trains were blocked, or spaced, twenty minutes apart. Each one required clearance papers after 7 p.m., one for the engineer and one for the conductor. These were inserted into wire clips in wooden hoops with long handles. The operator stood close to the track. The train slowed, and hoops were passed by hand to the engineer and to the conductor standing on the steps of the caboose. The train picked up speed at once and the empty hoops were hurled into the night far from the station. The operator had to go down the lonely track to search for them by lantern light.

"Did you find all your hoops last night?" Gray asked her one afternoon when she got up from her sleep. We helped her by scouting the track when she missed some.

"Shh," she said. "Let's go for a walk and I'll tell you a secret."

"I have a new system," Daisy confided. "I stand right next to the track with the clearance flat against my hand like this and my arm raised. The paper is flimsy and the wind from the train holds it there. The engineer and conductor reach out and brush palms with me and they each get their clearance in a flash. No more hoops!"

"Daisy, you'll get killed!" I said.

"No, I won't. The wind from the train keeps me in place, too. Now, don't you tell!"

We kept her secret and she used that system until a superintendent caught her when she was working in Dryden. Daisy earned $140 a month at first and later twice that amount plus overtime. This was big money.

In the spring of 1918 we added a separate kitchen to our house and another bedroom so that the Anglican ministers who stayed with us twice a month could have some privacy.

Our favourite clergyman during the war years was Canon Lofthouse,[10] who came down from Kenora before there was a circuit minister residing in Ignace, fifty miles to the east. He had been a bantam-weight boxing champion during his student days and he gave Gray and me lessons in the sport in our pyjamas. It was funny to hear this man of the cloth say, "Put up your dukes!" We told the other kids that our little minister could knock the hell out of you in the ring *and* in the pulpit.

Father was lay reader for the services and Clarence played the old pump organ. First Gray and then I became churchwardens as we grew older. Duties included cutting wood and rising early on winter Sundays to walk a mile down the track and build a fire in the church stove that had been cold for two weeks in sub-zero temperatures. Then there was the trek to the homestead for breakfast and back again to the church with the minister and our family. The last hike – to our house for lunch – seemed more like ten miles than one.

Except for the Rhinds, only four or five people came to church. Many times, as I took off my mitts to blow on numb fingers, it occurred to me that it would be easier to hold services in our home. My parents would not have agreed with me. The church was God's house and fighting bitter winds to get there strengthened the spirit.

The ill wind of winter blew good luck in Taffy Jones's direction one year. An Indian bought a Shetland pony and hitched it to his toboggan in place of the dog team. This worked fine until the snow in the bush became too deep for the pony. Still, ownership of horseflesh was a status symbol and another Indian called Isaac Chief was determined to have one, too. Since the Hudson's Bay Company was paying good money for furs, Isaac proposed to buy Taffy's horse, Prince. Taffy said, "No sale, I need him for hauling wood." Isaac persisted. Taffy named an outlandish price in order to settle the matter. But Isaac pulled a wad of bills from his pocket and paid on the spot.

Then he said, "I can't use him right now, the snow's too deep in the bush, so you take care of him while I'm on my trap line." They agreed on a monthly rate for hay and oats and the Indian paid two months in advance. When he turned up in the spring to claim the horse, Taffy said, "Hold on, you owe me three months board money."

Isaac said, "I won't pay more money. I got no use for that horse now anyway. You keep him and we'll call it square." So ended the best deal Taffy ever made in his life.

8

SKIRTING THE LAW

One day during our first summer on the homestead we chopped out a trail to the Jones place. They lived half a mile to the west on McKenzie Creek. Even if we had had a canoe we couldn't have travelled by water; the creek was a tangle of fallen trees and beaver dams.

A small man with a moustache like a worn shoe brush, Taffy Jones moved like a puppet in a Punch and Judy show with a definite list to the left. He hauled freight from the station to the Hudson's Bay store with a wagon and his black workhorse, Prince. On this day we reached the Jones place just as Taffy emerged from the barn with a pail of oats in one hand and a halter in the other.

"Well, lads," he said. "It's high time you came to see us. I'm just going out to look for Prince. Want to come along?" The horse grazed within a half-mile radius of the house but we found him after twenty minutes, his nose deep in the grass. He ignored us completely.

"Come on, Prince," Taffy wheedled. "See the nice feed I have for you." The horse rolled one eye in our direction. No fool, he knew a halter when he saw one. Prince continued to graze until Taffy was almost close enough to grab him. Then, placing one hoof languidly in front of the other, he moved a few steps out of reach and nibbled once more at the grass. Again and again he eluded capture with a minimum of effort until we reached the village.

Lorne Johnson, Bill Milroy, Mike Zoccole and others crowded the steps of the Hudson's Bay store. Cries of "Attaboy, Prince!" and "Go get 'im, Taffy," drew more spectators. As the cheers rose to a crescendo Taffy gave up and started for home, his face mottled and his jerky gait now a zigzag stagger. Prince followed meekly like the obedient horse he was not.

This scene was to be played many times, but the fun was over for today. We went home for our berry pails.

"Look in the swamp for red currants," mother said. "I want to make some jelly." There was a patch waiting for us. I popped one onto my tongue and pungent gall like the stink of a skunk flooded my mouth.

"What's wrong with you?" Gray asked as I spat and gasped and scrubbed my tongue on my sleeve. After that we learned to pick out the skunkberries by the fine hairs they bore. Otherwise they were identical to red currants.

Berries, fish and wild meat were principal items around the dinner-tables of Dinorwic. Mr. Martin, the game warden, bent the law for people living off the land. Travelling on the caboose at the back of a freight train, he was supposed to take people by surprise. However, he kept a ritual that allowed time for an out-of-season catch to be concealed. His first stop was always the Hudson's Bay store where he chatted with the manager for an hour or so. Meanwhile, Clarence slipped out the back door and hurried to the school.

When he tapped on the door and then opened it, the teacher said, "Class dismissed." Pupils ran home to warn their parents that the warden was in town. When he visited a settler's home he found merely a pot of tea and a plate of scones. Only when an infraction of the law was reported did he make a point of investigating.

In the spring, pickerel ran up McKenzie Creek by the thousands, heading for a waterfall to the north where they spawned. This was before the fishing season, but we speared some and smoked them for later use. Once when the pickerel were running Mr. Martin came to our house.

"I'm sorry to bother you, Mr. Rhind, but I've received a complaint that someone is netting fish and feeding them to their dogs."

"Indeed, sir," Father said. "We did *spear* a few but we certainly are not feeding them to the dogs!" Besides old Jack, we had two dogs that we had trained the previous winter to pull a sleigh loaded with hundred-pound sacks of flour and sugar. At that moment they were feasting on the box of smoked fish hidden under a pile of brush. Father didn't know they had broken loose. Mr. Martin accepted his statement and went to look for another culprit.

"What are you doing?" I asked when Mother fed twine into a small contraption with a wheel inside. On the table lay a number of coarse squares knotted together.

"Making fish nets," she said without looking up. Netting fish was illegal, but we made much better hauls with Mother's handiwork than we had with wooden spears. Without comment, our parents made adjustments between their Christian principles and the small crimes necessary for survival.

Jim Isbester taught us how to hide our moosemeat. "Just put it into a sack," he said, "and heave it into the bush like this." The sack sailed into the underbrush and sank beneath the snow. "This way there's no tracks," he said. We used that trick more than once.

During Prohibition[11] people made home brew and wine in Dinorwic as they did everywhere else. At that time a teacher called Miss Johnson boarded at the Quinn's hotel. She had come to us from Waldhof, where most of the settlers were German. Miss Johnson thought she was surrounded by the enemy and feared for her life. She was happier in Dinorwic, especially after she met George Kerr, a trapper and woodsman who lived at the hotel. Although he didn't return her affection she stayed on after school closed for the summer. Miss Johnson spent a lot of time out of doors. With her broad rump in the air and her ragged straw hat close to the ground she heaped a basket with yellow blooms.

"What's she doing with all those dandelions?" I asked Mr. Quinn.

"Bless you, son, she's making this and lots of it!" he said, tipping a jug full of liquid sunshine and taking a hearty swig. "One of these days she'll get old George drunk and then he'll be done for!"

"Why would she want to do that?"

"She's forty and on the shelf. She fancies George and he's not having any. Keep yer eyes open, Eric. This summer might get pretty hot."

"What do you mean?"

"Aw, yer too young, boy. Have a slug of this and don't ask so many questions." Not too tart, not too sweet, it was smooth on the tongue and warm in the stomach. I realized that this must be the stuff Mother took every night for medicinal purposes.

After my conversation with Mr. Quinn I noticed that whenever Miss Johnson came in the front door of the hotel, George went out the back. Then the seating arrangement for dinner was changed so that Miss Johnson sat next to her prey.

"Have some wine, Georgie," she would say, lifting the teapot that camouflaged her brew. George wore a chronic blush and his appetite declined as the summer wore on. Finally he moved to a small cabin on the edge of the nearby woods. He seldom showed up for meals.

A group of us, sitting on the hotel porch one still summer eve, heard Miss Johnson carolling "Georgie!" as she plodded up the trail to the cabin. It had only one door and we pictured him squeezing through the back window. He must have, because Miss Johnson returned to the hotel within minutes, clutching a jug to her breast.

George grew thinner. One day he braved the teacher's amorous glances for the sake of Mrs. Quinn's cooking and the company of other diners. During the meal Bill Milroy glanced out the window and saw a Mountie[12] approaching. "Here comes the law!" he said.

"My wine, my wine, he's after me!" Miss Johnson wailed. Steps shook as she thundered up the stairs to her bedroom.

"Come on, fellows, let's help her get rid of it," Bill said. Safe in the group, George went along and I followed. The bedroom door was open. There she stood, pouring a shining stream from a large jug into the china chamber-pot.

"It's too small, it's too small!" she cried as the wine reached the lip of the container.

"Don't worry," Bill said. "We'll drink the rest of it."

"No, no, he'll be up here any minute!" She shoved the pot under the bed and made for the next bedroom. In no time the evidence was safely stowed under the beds. Except for the jug. Miss Johnson looked frantically around the room. The green netting tacked over the open window bulged and then ripped as she shoved the jug through to land "plop" in the flowerbed below.

She patted her hair, jerked at her skirt and moved slowly

down the stairs like a proper schoolmarm. Weak from laughter, the rest of us followed.

The officer was having tea with Mrs. Quinn.

"You folks seem to have a jolly time here," he said. "Wish I could stay the night. But I just stopped off to visit; have to catch the next freight out."

The teacher's face turned the colour of suet; she dropped into a chair. A few days later she left Dinorwic forever. It wasn't the disgrace of having men see her chamber-pot that finished her. It was the bitter knowledge that George Kerr, lured to her bedroom at last, was part of a comedy the village would never forget. The point of the episode was lost on me at the time. Mr. Quinn was right, I was too young. George Kerr moved back to the hotel and later married Violet, only daughter of the Isbesters.

During these years, temperance workers travelled in pairs to hold propaganda meetings in towns and villages. Such gatherings were regarded as free entertainment in Dinorwic. When the notice was posted for the first time I hiked over to the Lawrence's to make sure they knew about it.

The day was cold, the door closed. When Mrs. Lawrence let me in, feathers drifted across the floor in the sudden draft. A shrill squawking hampered our conversation.

"They're not usually so noisy," Mrs. Lawrence said. "Maybe they don't like strangers. Have you tried keeping your chickens inside? It's nice to have eggs for breakfast without going out in the cold." When I told her about the meeting she said she would be there with bells on.

Every seat in the schoolhouse was taken that night and people leaned against the walls. The speakers took turns waving their arms and pounding on the desk. People who would be tending their stills in the morning were close to tears at the pictures of ruin and disgrace drawn for them with word and gesture.

At the close of the evening a collection was taken to defray expenses. "What did you think of the meeting?" Mother asked Mrs. Lawrence.

"It was real good!" she said. "I put a dollar on the plate so's they could buy a bottle. They must be real thirsty after all that yelling."

9

NO BULL

On a blue and gold summer morning I sat on a box outside the open window of the Men's Room at the hotel. "How many kids you got now?" Bill asked Mr. Lawrence, who was visiting his family that week.

"I dunno, every time I come home there's a new one. They never stand still long enough so's I can count 'em."

Another voice said, "Yer a real stud, Jack," and they all laughed. Grown-ups made strange jokes, I thought. The only studs I knew of belonged to collars. I couldn't ask Mother or Father what this meant. They wouldn't approve of my eavesdropping. Maybe Mrs. Lawrence could explain.

I found her in the garden hoeing potatoes. There was a mound nearby with a little fence around it. "Is that a cucumber bed?" I asked.

"Oh, no," she said. "I buried Satan there, the baby that died last week. It's a shame, I'd picked out such a nice name for him." I forgot about the stud problem. If Satan had survived, I wondered, would he have lived up to his name?

All her boys were devils, in my opinion. Once I saw four of them racing around their clearing with long cords attached to the legs of weakly flapping blackbirds. Against the bright summer sky, blue-black bodies sank with each flutter like kites when the wind dies away. The open beaks were silent. So were the boys. Heads back, they played the cords, running here and there, trampling the amputated birds' feet strewn on the ground. My stomach churned and I ran for home.

"Eric, what's the matter?" Mother asked.

"It's Peter; and Tom. They're using blackbirds for kites and the feet..." Mother waited until I could tell the rest of the story.

"I'll see what I can do," she said. Mrs. Lawrence was pleased to have a visitor but astonished by Mother's mission.

"What's wrong with it? The boys are having a good time." However, having reason to be grateful for her guest's services as a midwife, she agreed to end the game.

Mother had not always been adept at midwifery – she added it to her skills after settling in Canada. She hadn't even admitted to her own pregnancies until she went into labour, a Victorian modesty that enraged her physician. In Dinorwic, medical necessity and the desire to help others overcame her earlier reticence. One of the Lawrence girls came to our place for help each time a new brother or sister was ready to join the brood. We got no details from Mother. All she ever said was that she wished there were a real chair in that house. She never quite got used to sitting on a block of wood.

There was nobody to ask about the mystery of human reproduction. Even Daisy, always eager to instruct her little brothers, would say nothing on this subject. We knew that somehow a bull caused a cow to have a calf, but there was no bull in Dinorwic. When the time was ripe an animal owned by the government was shipped to various points on the railway division and there people took their cows.

When Daisy was the night operator in Dryden, this message came over the wire: "Call agent get section men out. Bull arrives 11 p.m. freight." Mr. Campbell, the agent, was not at home. The assistant agent did not have a telephone. Daisy had to get permission from the dispatcher in Kenora to leave the building and go to the man's house. Because of her Victorian upbringing she shied away from the word "bull," which was too suggestive to be spoken by a nice girl when talking with a man. As she explained the situation she substituted the words "gentleman cow."

By the time she had the assistant agent in tow the train was in. Since it was too late to round up the section men, the train moved on without the bull being given an opportunity to do his duty. Before leaving, however, the bull's custodians demanded that a message be sent to Ignace informing the section men there that they soon would be needed. On the telegraph key, Daisy reported the imminent arrival of a gentleman cow to Ignace. When it arrived the section men refused to unload it because it was billed to Dryden. The bull went on to Fort William, and returned to Dryden the following night. By this time everyone on the division was in stitches. Brakemen and conductors chuckled when they saw Daisy. "Hear you had a problem last night," they said. "*What* kind of cow did you say that was?"

"I've never been so embarrassed," she said when she related the story at Creekside.

By now, Gray and I had a pretty good idea what this was all about but we needed to have our suspicion confirmed. We couldn't be sure how cows and bulls procreated, and as for humans – Mother and Father? It seemed incredible. I thought I would begin with cattle and try to get information from Father. I tagged along when he walked to the store for tobacco.

"Father, do bulls have calves?"

"No, Eric, they don't."

"Do they give milk?"

"No, they do not."

"Then what *are* they good for?"

"Bulls are for breeding purposes." He pulled his pipe from his pocket, stuck it unlit into his mouth and walked on so rapidly that it was hard to keep up with him. I had already sensed that Father felt inadequate now and then. This was one of those times. Intimate conversation was not in his line. Apparently he decided to compensate for this deficiency by taking a more active role around the homestead.

One of the duties Gray and I had was to kill a chicken or a surplus rooster for Sunday dinner. The first time we undertook this job, we placed the bird on a block of wood on its back and I held the feet. Gray swung the axe high. The victim blinked at me with little round eyes. At the crucial moment I let go, the bird escaped and the axe split the block in two.

"What in blazes did you do that for?" Gray asked.

"I couldn't stand the way it looked at me."

"Well, you'll just have to catch it. We have to eat, don't we?"

The next time the axe descended I closed my eyes and held

on. Thwack! The severed head lay on the ground, still blinking. The body ran in circles round the yard. I never liked these executions but the chicken dinners that followed were worth a few squeamish moments.

However, all was not well with the flock. By whatever reasoning bird brains employ, one of the group was declared an outcast. The others pecked it incessantly and chased it away at feeding time. It was skinny, bald and half naked. The day Father declined to explain the function of bulls was the day Mother chose to release the persecuted chicken from its misery.

"Do it now, boys, and get it over with," she said. Father looked up from his book.

"I shall attend to it, Lizzie," he said. Mother stared as he rose from his chair.

"How, Willie?" she asked. She couldn't see Father with an axe and a struggling chicken.

"I'll shoot it," he said firmly, reaching for the rifle on the wall. This was a big gun capable of felling a moose. Gray and I kept straight faces but we couldn't wait to see the chicken explode.

We lurked near the spot where the condemned was hiding from its tormentors. Father marched into view with the rifle under one arm and the chicken under the other. When he went behind the stable we peeked around the corner of the building. Father put the chicken on the ground. Backed up three feet. Went down on one knee; put the gun to his shoulder. We tensed, waiting for the bang. The scraggly bird hopped up to the rifle, cocked its bald head and peered down the gun barrel. There was absolute silence. Then Father stood up, holding the chicken. He walked slowly to the chicken coop and released it. He unloaded the big rifle and trudged back to the house. We stayed out of sight.

This was a father we had never seen before and from that day we loved him more. Soon we began to call him Dad and he seemed to like this.

He was more successful at baking bread and rolls. His yeast was made from potatoes, flour, salt, sugar, water and two dry yeast cakes. This was left in a pot and never allowed to run out. The dough rose in the daytime and Dad baked at night when he had the kitchen to himself. He read and smoked his pipe while the loaves cooked. The aroma drifted to our room and Gray and I woke up, drooling at the thought of fluffy white rolls, their glazed brown tops spread like umbrellas. When Dad was lost in his book we crept out and snatched one each.

While Daisy worked as relief operator in lonely places like Hawk Lake she always knew when the family had fresh bread. The railroad track ran close to our house and train crews were aware that the lady operator's home was Creekside. If they saw lights on late at night they told Daisy, "Your Dad was baking bread last night," and she thought of the family at breakfast, the crusty loaves on the table and her own chair next to Mother's.

10

GAME FOR ANYTHING

Daisy was lonely at Hawk Lake. The only dwellings besides the station house were the pumphouse and the section house. The only other woman was the section foreman's wife, who spoke little English. My sister asked me to visit her. There was no station agent there; Daisy was in charge during the day and at night the Kenora despatcher operated without the assistance of Hawk Lake.

Her living quarters were the bedroom and the office. The previous operator had been a bachelor and the kitchen was a

Daisy with coal scuttles.

wasteland. Pots and pans overflowing the sink held a garden of blue and yellow mould. Crusted and furry dishes hid the table. Cobwebs glimmered in the faint light from the grubby window. Daisy had locked the door on the foul scene and used the office stove for cooking. I carried coal for her and cleaned the lamps and lanterns. Before darkness fell Daisy climbed a ladder and placed a lantern to show up the signal. The signal board rose high above the station. Each of its arms had a movable section with red and green discs. The green always showed until the signal arm was dropped by unclipping the chain over the operator's desk.[13] Electricity for the key was supplied by a storage battery which was checked at intervals by linemen.

Signal board at Wabigoon station, with William Rhind
standing in front of the operator's outset window.

Surrounded by rock, Hawk Lake was a prime target during a thunder and lightning storm. It sounded as though the rocks had parted into giant balls that were thundering down to crash on the station roof. Blue lights danced on the iron stove, jagged beams shot to the ground outside. Once, when Daisy got up from her chair for a better look, lightning struck the key and scorched the pad on her desk.

There were other dangers. Even in wartime, men rode the rails. Eluding the law in Kenora, they would get as far as Hawk Lake where trains stopped at night for water. More than once, we were awakened by tramps trying the door. I thought my sister was very brave to stay in this creepy place.

On her day off she took me to Eagle River. We boarded the caboose on the back of a freight and the conductor let me ride in the cupola, a small square look-out on the top of the caboose. Here I could see the full length of the train. A freight coming from the opposite direction looked as though it would hit us head-on. As the boxcars swayed past they seemed to miss us by inches.

I wanted to ride in an engine. The railway track was our road to the homestead and I formed the habit of walking past the locomotive when a local train stood in the station. At last the engineer leaned out of his cab and said, "Going home, son? Climb aboard and I'll drop you off at Creekside." I was small for my age and he put me in front of him on the seat. With my head out the window I watched the rails slide away behind us. When the fireman opened the firebox the scorching heat of the blaze made me think of the fires of hell.

High in the great black beast I felt her power all through my body. As we drew near Creekside the engineer said, "Here, pull the whistle cord, lad." I gave it a mighty yank and the wail shivered to my toes. "I'm going to be an engineer when I grow up," I said when the train stopped at the homestead.

"That's a fine idea, son, but first you'll have to be a fireman." There ended one ambition; that firebox was too hot for me.

Daisy often rode the freights. Operators were allowed to travel on them to a new job or to go home for time off. She slept on the bunk in the cupola and train men shared their lunch with her. She was in the baggage car one day at lunch time when a train man began to spread newspapers on a long wooden box on the floor of the car. "We're having lunch on Joe today," he said, arranging thick sandwiches and rosy apples on the newspapers.

"Joe...?" Daisy said. The baggage man grinned and gestured at the pine box that so often served, in those days, as a coffin. Daisy ate her lunch and passed another test that had nothing to do with the rule book.

When the freight train slowed at Creekside she hit the ground running to avoid broken bones. She bounced into the house and said, "Mother, where are the snapshot albums?" Daisy still yearned for Hereford and she didn't want Gray and me to forget the life we had had there.

"That's Win holding the bicycle in front of our old house and that's you, Eric, perched on the seat." The girl in the picture smiled, her hair streamed to her waist. Vines hung like curtains down each side of the window behind her. The toddler wore a white dress.

Win and Eric at Hereford, 1907.

"That's not me!" I said.

"Yes, it is, even boys wore dresses then." Another photo showed a group on a lawn smooth as a carpet with a yew tree on one side. There was Mother, slim in a gored skirt and frilly blouse. Daisy looked about six. A white lace collar covered her shoulders; both hands held a croquet mallet poised to strike the ball. Father stood tall and easy in a dark suit, his watch-chain prominent on his waistcoat.

The Rhind family in Hereford: Eliza (standing left in white blouse), Daisy, 6, baby Gray, Win, William.

Mother left the room and returned with a miniature of Dr. Rhind that we had seen before. This time I studied the image of my grandfather. Pale chiseled face; smooth red hair; a velvet cravat; low on the green brocade waistcoat something hung on a cord.

"What is that?" I asked.

"The family seal," Mother said. "People used to seal the backs of their letters so they could only be opened by the person they were addressed to. I still have that seal, and a stick of red wax."

Gray was bored. He went outside to split wood. Daisy closed the album and said, "Mother, I'd like to talk to you. Gray is almost fourteen and I want to send him to high school in Dryden. I'll pay for his room and board and any books and clothes that he'll need."

Outside the window, Gray's axe rose and fell. Mother watched for a moment. Then she turned to Daisy and said quietly,

"We can't spare him, I'm afraid. You know Father isn't strong. There is so much land to clear yet – and all the chores – we need him here." She went out to her flowerbed without another word.

"I think Mother is bushed," Daisy said. And I thought, if Gray can't go to high school then it's a sure thing I can't either. For the first time I faced the possibility of spending my whole life in Dinorwic. Daisy said, "She always talked of a future for her boys. I thought that was why we came to Canada."

I went outside with Daisy. Mother was picking dead flowers from the pink and white sweet peas blooming on a trellis. We watched as though her busy fingers might give us a clue to her thoughts. Had she buried all her dreams? Did the gracious home in Hereford seem like a fantasy now? It did to me. My eight years there were like a favourite story remembered. In that story Mother gardened in a sun-bonnet. Her face was pink and white and her crown of chestnut hair her one vanity. Now her skin was brown and deeply seamed, her hair pulled back in a tight gray knot. The essentials of survival concerned her now, although the droll streak in her nature popped out now and then like a white rabbit from a black hat.

Once she posed for the camera dressed as an Ojibway woman with a pipe in her mouth, then photographed Clarence with the wife of an Indian chief. On the back of this she wrote, "Clarence and his bride." Both snapshots went to England in a letter to a friend.

Mother introduced adult participation in school concerts by writing and acting in a skit based on old ladies' gossiping. This was natural material because of her passionate interest in people and all the details of their lives. She knew everything that happened in Dinorwic and passed on the latest reports without delay. We had no newspaper then. When we did receive a regular paper from Fort William, Mother inhaled the aroma of printer's ink as though it were perfume. She never settled down to a read without first sniffing the front page. But before the newspaper entered our lives the bush was our world and events in Dinorwic were second only to news of the great battles of the war.

We all knew that Rosie Jones and Zeke Lawrence were furnishing a house but no date had been set for the wedding. One hot June morning when Daisy was at home Mother said, "They're getting married today. Will you please take this parcel to the Jones's place?" She had crocheted a set of doilies for Rosie.

"They left today," Mrs. Jones said. "Went to Dryden to tie the knot. They'll be gone for a week."

Several days later Zeke knocked on the door at Creekside and opened it without waiting for an answer. "Me and Rosie just got back," he said, "and all our furniture's gone! So are Abe and Sam, the buggers. They'll be sorry when the Mounties get here! Did you folks see anything?"

When the Mountie assigned to the case arrived in Dinorwic he learned that two of the Lawrence boys (now mysteriously absent from the scene) had been observed driving a wagon loaded with furniture. Gray and I directed the officer to their homestead and hid in the bush to watch. There was nothing unusual in the barn. The officer paced the clearing and stopped suddenly beside a haystack. He poked it with a stick, then thrust an arm in and pulled out a chair. A kitchen table came next. "Hey," said Mrs. Lawrence, appearing at his elbow with Esther and Ruth, "me and the girls will give you a hand."

Mrs. Lawrence told Mother later, "Such a nice policeman paid us a visit. He even took our pictures!" In the end, no charges were laid.

That summer I noticed a change in Mr. Quinn, He had always been game for anything, from naughts and crosses to a walk in the woods. Now he said, "Maybe tomorrow, Eric. I'm a bit fagged today." He had always reminded me of a teddy bear. Now he had lost some of his stuffing. When he took to his bed a few months later all Dinorwic knew he was dying. Mother went straight to Quinn's hotel.

"He wants to see you, Eric," she said later. My heart bumped all the way to the hotel. It was thrashing by the time I climbed the stairs to the room where he lay – so still, so flat! – a waxworks figure nothing like the jolly Mr. Quinn with the golden wine flowing from an upturned bottle down to his broad belly.

I thought I was too late and backed slowly to the door. But I could not take my gaze from that still, gray face and so I saw the eyelids lift a fraction and heard him whisper, "Eric." I went to the bed and took his cold fingers in mine. They moved slightly and then his eyes closed and I knew that they would not open again. I wished that I knew what he had wanted to tell me. As I backed to the door again my heart slowed to a sickening lurch but I managed to run down the stairs and out the door.

Daisy was home on holiday so she took me to Port Arthur to cheer me up. I saw my first picture show. It was a silent movie. The actors jerked their way through a love scene that made no sense to me. The star put his arm around the leading lady and bent his head to hers. "Why is he smelling her hair?" I said aloud to Daisy.

"SHH!" she answered.

It was years before I saw another movie. This was no hardship. I knew *real* people who talked and swore at their horses and buried babies in the backyard.

Kathleen Quinn went away to school around 1919, so Gray and I didn't miss her much when she and her mother left Dinorwic. Charles and Lillie Guay took over the hotel. Mrs. Guay was a lively dark-eyed lady who was equal to any situation. She placed an illicit partridge dinner on the table one day just as the game warden walked in.

"Mr. Martin, You must join us," she said. "Nobody can resist our fried rabbit." The game warden ate heartily.

When he pushed back his chair he said, "That was delicious, Mrs. Guay. Now tell me, what sort of tree did you find those rabbits in?"

11

CHRISTMAS CONCERT

For entertainment value and sheer festivity, nothing compared to the annual Christmas concert held in the schoolhouse. It was strange and exciting, going to school at night. The grown-ups went too, wearing polished Sunday boots that squeaked on the path instead of the everyday winter footwear made of black felt or deerhide moccasins lined with fur. The lamp on the inside window sill cast a soft reflection on the snow.

Inside, kitchen chairs borrowed from every household lined the walls but some people had to sit awkwardly in desks too small for them. Many of the ladies were able to squeeze skirts and lisle-clad ankles under the desk tops, but long legs attired in black serge trousers or blue overalls projected here and there into the aisles. Odours of chalk dust, split wood and old smoke in our schoolroom were overpowered by a sharp piney smell that tingled our nostrils. The evergreen was too large for the room but just right for the occasion; the star on top touched the ceiling; thrusting branches shimmered with tinsel. Soon candles clamped to lower branches would be lighted one by one to flicker and glow on the tips of the tree's green arms. Father, now a school trustee, would stand guard with a pail of water. I hoped he wouldn't have to use it for there were presents under the tree: books and knitted mufflers and chocolate fudge and perhaps a surprise or two.

Father Christmas had come back into our lives. Now called Santa Claus, he was Mr. Isbester dressed in a red suit and black rubber boots. Since his beard was cotton batten, the dancing candlelight was extinguished before he bent to distribute the presents. There had been an accident in Wabigoon one time when

Santa's beard ignited and he was badly burned.

Although there was no mystery for Gray and me concerning Santa, his appearance was the highlight of the concert. During the concert in 1916 we glanced often at the door of the school. Mr. Isbester was late. He and his son-in-law, George Kerr, were staying in the trapping shack on Big Sandy Lake but they had promised to come in for the concert. Mr. Isbester liked to see the performance before retiring to the cloakroom to don his costume.

The teacher's desk had been pushed aside to allow for a stage. In the centre of the space that night Mother was reciting. She had curled her hair with tongs heated in the lamp-chimney and dolled herself up in a long skirt and cream silk blouse that usually lay in her trunk. Her audience was laughing when cold air swept in from the back of the room. George Kerr sagged against the door-frame. He looked old and sick and he was shivering. People jumped from their seats and pulled George into the room. Someone closed the door and asked, "What happened? Where's Jim?"

George swallowed, looked around the encircling faces and said, "I tried my damndest. Weak spot in the ice. Jim was hanging onto the edge of the hole when I caught up. He said 'Get me a pole.' His lips blue already. The load was soaked and the whole shebang going down. Jim's dogs. Backward into the water. Snarling and fighting. My dogs got their hackles up. Kept them out of it somehow. The island – heavy branch. Back in a minute. Just one minute!" George shuddered. He clenched his teeth on the sobs and said, "Nothing. Nothing there but the black hole in the ice."

He looked around for Violet, his wife and Jim's daughter. She had already slipped by the group and gone to her mother. The Christmas concert was over, and Christmas itself was not merry that year for anyone over the age of six.

12

DELIRIUM

In 1918 the Spanish flu struck Canada. Daisy was inoculated with the rest of the CPR employees but the serum was ineffective. While in Kenora in the fall of 1918 she contracted the disease. Hospitals were full and public buildings such as the library were jammed with the sick and the dying. The doctor who saw Daisy told her landlady that his patient did not have the flu. Otherwise she would have been evicted and there was literally no place for her to go. By November 1918 she was convalescent but too weak to join the people who thronged the streets to celebrate the Armistice.

The disease hit Dinorwic early in 1919. Its onset was so sudden that brawny men who worked at full strength in the morning collapsed like rag dolls in the afternoon. Except for Father, the Rhinds fell to the disease one by one. Clarence developed it first and came home to be nursed. Then Gray and I sickened, and, last of all, Mother.

The victims had high fevers, drenching sweats, swollen tongues and nosebleeds. There was no running water, no inside toilet and no washing-machine in the house. Kleenex had not yet been invented. We used rags that Father soaked in cold water and salt to remove the blood and mucous, then boiled to kill the infection. Supposedly so delicate, he cared for us all and went daily to the Jones homestead to feed Prince. Taffy and his wife were flat on their backs.

Daisy asked the CPR doctor to see us on his rounds. He came with quinine tablets and brandy – there was no other medication available to fight this terrible sickness. Two of those who died were Violet Kerr and Jim Williams, the friend who had taught Gray and me to skin a weasel. It was weeks before I knew this; I was fighting double pneumonia.

The chills that shook the bed, the blazing fever and Father's bent figure all faded away. I was seven years old again, running from the garden in Hereford with a bowl in my hand. The clattering cart stopped. The salt man broke chunks from a block and rubbed them between his hands. Fine salt sprayed into my dish. The crumpet lady arrived with her wares in a cloth-covered basket. Then it was night. I waited by the gate for the lamplighter. Street lamps flared one by one as he poked a long pole into the bottom of each gaslight on its tall standard. I watched until he turned the corner at the end of the street.

It was Sunday. We hiked in the Dinedor Hills. Gray and I wore white suits. Mother and Daisy had shiny straw hats banded with flowers. Father carried his walking-stick with the silver knob. We came to the tea garden halfway up the highest hill. China gleamed on small tables set under spreading branches and ladies in long aprons served tea and ginger beer.

When I opened my eyes Daisy was sitting beside the bed. A dispatcher named Howard Sharpe had given up his holidays so she could come home to help Dad. He was exhausted and there was not a clean towel or dish in the house. Mother's temperature was 104 degrees.

We were lucky. By March 1919, Daisy's twenty-first birthday, everyone was recovering. That day a telegram came ordering Daisy back to work. As she was packing, the back door opened and a stranger walked into the kitchen, hesitating just inside the door. His khaki pants hung loose. Dark hair touched the collar of a faded shirt and straggled down his forehead. Slowly he raised a hand to brush it from tired brown eyes.

"Bertie!" Mother cried. Curled up on the couch under an afghan, she struggled to get up. It really was my brother, an altered Bert who moved slowly and frowned when Daisy sobbed on his shoulder, clutching him like a lost treasure. He pulled away.

"I say, wot's all this bawling?" he said. "I'm 'ere, ain't I?" Father's eyebrows shot up and I could follow his thoughts. What sort of persons had Bert spent the last four years with? Mother was oblivious to flaws in the reunion.

Still weak from the flu, she began to pull pots and pans from the cupboard.

"Sit down, Lizzie," Father said. "I'll get the dinner." Daisy dried her eyes and finished packing.

Bert's behaviour was odd for weeks. We would find him in the morning curled up on the floor under the kitchen table. At mealtimes he often went for a walk instead of sitting down with the family. He spent the day reading, a book on the table in front of him and the tops of his large ears folded down, apparently to shut out sound. This was his way of saying leave me alone.

When buds appeared on the trees he emerged from withdrawal and helped Gray and me clear land. His pallor disappeared and once more his eyes twinkled with fun or blazed with emotion. One day we were chopping underbrush and laughing over the story of Miss Johnson. "Mother says we should have an annual picnic in her honour and serve dandelion wine in miniature chamber pots," I said. "The trouble is, the Bay doesn't stock such an item. Neither does Eaton's catalogue."

"You're pulling our leg," Gray said.

"Well, she didn't actually say it to *me*. I just happened to hear her talking to Dad. Say, Bert," I went on, to change the subject, "tell us about the prison camp." Bert hurled his axe into the bush and bolted from the clearing. We watched him vanish around the sharp curve in the railway track.

A few days later I sat on a log with Bert while he rolled a smoke. He tamped the tobacco evenly in the small white paper, licked the edges and finished with a quick twist of his fingers. Unlit, the cigarette drooped from his hand. At last he spoke.

"If you really want to know, it was bloody 'ell. First off they shoved all the Canadian prisoners on a cattle train. No proper walls to the cars, just wooden slats. Cold as Siberia, no food, no toilets. Paraded through Germany like a bunch of circus animals. People crowded the platform at every town. Women came up to the cars with food in their hands. We reached through the slats and they snatched it away. They even spat at us. They really hated Canadians. So did the guards at the camp in Munster. When a fellow collapsed with the Spanish flu, they kicked him until he got up. Died like flies in that place. The guards took our food parcels and kept them until the food was mouldy.

"As soon as we got to the camp they sent us to work in a coal mine. One day a chap refused to go into the mine. Two guards grabbed him and threw him down the shaft. Maybe he was better off, dyin' like that. It was horrible, slaving in that damp black pit and always hungry. You didn't care if you lived or died. One morning I refused to go down. An officer drew his revolver and pulled the trigger. Nothing happened. 'You're one hell of a soldier,' I said, 'can't even keep your gun loaded.' My German wasn't up to much then; guess he didn't understand me. But saying that perked me up and I went down the hole for another day.

"Men would try anything to get out of that mine. One fellow set his foot on the rail that carried the coal cars. Crushed to a bloody pulp it was, and got him into hospital for a nice long rest."

Bert shivered in the June sunshine. "Go on," I said.

"Enough of this jabberin'," he said. "Let's get on with it."

Years later I heard that the German soldiers' hatred for Canadians stemmed from the belief that our soldiers were mercenaries, soldiers without honour who fought for money.

13

THE COW, THE HORSE
AND THE WOLF

With his separation pay from the army, Bert bought a cow. After a visit to the government bull stationed in Wabigoon, she eventually produced a calf. Gray and I thought we understood the process now, at least as it related to cows and bulls.

One day while hoeing in the garden I looked up as the westbound train whistled at the curve. Our calf was on the rails, the cow following. The cow stopped and faced the oncoming train like a mouse defying a lion. A gory mess flew into the air and rolled down the embankment. Sickened, I ran to save the calf before another train came along. Later, section men gathered up Bessie's remains and buried her near the track. I wished they hadn't, for I had to pass the mound every day.

Bert bought another cow and soon we had surplus milk to sell to Mrs. Johnson, wife of the new store manager. She paid ten cents a quart for it. I carried it down the track in lard pails, battling wind and temperatures that often fell to forty below zero. Since my hands were full with milk and school-books, my nose was usually frozen by the time I reached the store. So was the milk and Mrs. Johnson was not pleased.

The cow was milked early in the morning. In warm weather we had to find her first. Cow and heifer grazed our clearing, then roamed the bush. Sometimes they went through Taffy's homestead and crossed his bridge over the creek. On other days we found them three miles from home on the old road to Big Sandy, which had been used when the Grand Trunk Pacific Railway was under construction. Taffy's place was on our side of the creek; the road to Big Sandy Lake was across the tracks on the opposite side. It was our chore to find the cows, so Gray and I went in different directions to listen for bells and watch for cowplasters.

Gray (left) and Eric haying.

Gray had completed the eighth grade and now worked on the track with Bert, so I had to finish the round-up and do the milking if these chores were not done before they went to work. In spring and fall I was usually late for school. "Your turn will come" had a new meaning now. I could look forward to hard labour on the section gang when the Dinorwic schoolhouse had no more to offer me.

During those years I grew so rapidly that hunger nagged me constantly. Mother left pans of milk in the back shed so that the cream used for making butter would rise to the top. I came in shaking with hunger and swallowed a pan of milk in a few gulps. This earned me some cross words but I was too happy about my spurt of growth to care. Eventually, at six feet, I could look down at the brothers who would always outrank me in the family.

Gray (left) and Eric after his growth spurt.

Meanwhile, Charlie Stanford, a fellow who returned to Dinorwic at the same time as Bert, visited Creekside often and the two of them reminisced about the war. One Saturday Bert took Gray and me to Charlie's homestead. The men drank home brew while Charlie related adventures from the days before the war when he travelled the world as a ship's cook. "Got into a lot of bloomers in those days," he said. For our benefit he supplied some details and our suspicions about the relations between men and women were confirmed at last.

We walked home, Bert chuckling to himself and Gray and I mulling over what we had learned. We greeted our parents with our everyday innocent faces. There was no question of discussing sex with them. Certain topics were never mentioned. Emotions were not to be expressed too vividly. Even the word "darn" was taboo. Dad said it was a substitute for damn and it was the desire to swear that counted. Our swearing was done at a safe distance from Creekside.

When I was fourteen we had a horse and a log stable on the homestead. Charlie Stanford kept his horse there and allowed us to use her when hauling pulpwood in the winter. Neither one was a workhorse and you could not have found a more poorly matched team in all of Canada. Charlie's mare was cranky and skittish. Our Bill was a slow plodder.

There were few horses in Dinorwic. I hitched up old Bill now and then to take a trapper to Big Sandy Lake. When someone wanted goods hauled to their homestead I did that too, on a rough bush trail. Half a day's work earned me a dollar and Dad's high praise: "Here's the boy who brings in the money!"

One winter I was on the old Gold Rock road with the team when a teenaged Indian girl ran through the bush toward me. "Help!" she said in English, already turning to dash back down the path with me behind her. We stopped at the door of a tiny shack on the bank of the lake. Inside, an ancient Ojibway woman lay dead on the floor, her bare feet inches from the red-hot tin heater. A small dog sprawled across her chest, whining.

The girl stood in silence, her dark eyes fixed on me. "I'll stay here," I said. "Go to the Hudson's Bay for help."

The dog continued to whine. "Better chuck him outside," I thought. But he evaded my hands, scrambled to a corner of the room, threw back his head and howled. I tried to estimate how long it would take the girl to cover the one-mile distance to the store and then back to the cabin. The eyes of the corpse stared up at the ceiling. With a blanket from the cot I covered her from bare toes to gray head. The dog howled.

At last the girl returned with two trappers who had come in for supplies. Delivered, I hurried down the trail to my wagon.

One fall I took a trapper to Big Sandy Lake. He didn't want to wait until there was snow for his dog team. We had to pass Frank Hazelwood's place. Although I hadn't seen him for some time I felt sure he would give us a cup of tea. He had always liked

Gray and me.

Hunters no longer stayed at Frank's for the season. It was rumoured that he was a little strange. I was thirsty and quite prepared to overlook a few quirks.

His cabin was locked and nobody answered my yell. As I hopped onto the wagon Frank appeared from behind his cabin with a rifle in his hand. He raised it and shot over my head.

Old Bill made it to the dock at a dead gallop. I had to stand up and pull savagely at the reins to make him stop. The trapper jumped into the waiting canoe. It rocked and then straightened out, leaping away from the dock like a startled deer. The mooring rope pulled loose from rotten wood and trailed behind like a long tail.

There was only one road back. Old Bill snorted and rolled his eyes. I had to slap his rump. When he moved, his pace was closer to a trot than the usual reluctant trudge. I crouched in the wagon, ready to jump if I saw the gun. There was no sign of Frank. Ragged green blinds hid the windows.

Usually I drove the two horses, Stanford's and ours, hitched to a bob-sleigh. This was two separate sleighs connected by crossed chains which equalized the pull and ensured that the back of the sleigh followed the front. Each section had runners four feet apart connected by a heavy timber. On each of these timbers lay a longer one called a bunk, fastened to the cross-piece with a steel pin. A rack of cordwood kept the conveyance rigid. When an empty bob-sleigh was in motion the bunks swung freely. A driver sitting on the front bunk fought to keep his place when the sleigh turned a corner.

Balancing on the edge of an empty pulpwood rack had its hazards too, as Taffy Jones discovered. Here and there on a winter road were slopes or slants caused by sleighs bunting the edge of a ploughed road and gradually widening it. Taffy was on his way home from the store one day, slapping the reins in a vain effort to change Prince's amble to a trot. They came to a spot where the road sloped to the side. Prince jumped forward, the sleigh jack-knifed into the slope and Taffy flew ass over tea-kettle into the snow bank. By the time he landed, Prince was galloping homeward.

On another day my team pulled me and the empty bob-sleigh on a bush road which was only as wide as the V-shaped wooden plow which had cleared it. High banks of snow rose on each side. I balanced on the front bunk, my axe driven into the wood. I was lost in one of the fantasies that drove away cold and boredom. There was a crimson rug dizzy with flowers on the office floor, just like the one we had had in the drawing-room in Hereford. With my feet on a polished desk I barked orders to an office boy who stood meekly at a respectful distance from me: THE BOSS.

My magic carpet dropped me with a thud onto the sleigh. Ahead raced the lone wolf I had seen loping down the railway track scavenging scraps from the dining-cars. Now his head turned from side to side, seeking escape from the sleigh that filled the road and carried the scent of man. If he jumped into the loose snow flanking the road he would be trapped. I could not turn the sleigh in the narrow space and the horses, aroused by the sight of the wild animal, began to gallop. The wolf ran faster, barely keeping his lead. We came to a spot where the uneven bush road sloped to the left. A streak of gray fur bolted onto the slope for safety. I grabbed my axe and swung for his head. He snapped at my wrist like a dog and I had a clear view of his fangs. The horses galloped. I slithered on the bunk. Sweat drenched me as we passed the wolf and went on.

That night it snowed again. Gray said at breakfast, "Let's see if we can get a shot at the brute." No sign of wolf tracks showed in the fresh snow. We went home for lunch and sat facing windows that overlooked the railway line. There was the lone wolf, sauntering along between the rails. I took the big rifle and Gray the 22. On top of our morning footprints lay the imprint of careful paws.

Gray said, "You take the railway and I'll go up the road." The wolf saw me and ran for the bush. Gray fired and missed. The fugitive leaped for the rails once more, slowed when he saw me and I got him. The provincial government paid me $15 bounty and I felt like a millionaire. Extra money eased the Rhind family budget, always stretched like a garter on a fat leg. There was no welfare assistance then, no unemployment insurance. Clarence helped to keep the family when we first came to Canada. When Daisy became a telegrapher she sent money home. But soon they would both be married.

14

GIVE ME YOUR ANSWER, DO

In May 1919 Canon Lofthouse married Clarence to Phoebe Wright in her family's big farmhouse southeast of Wabigoon not far from the shore of the lake. There was dancing later and a pile of presents to open. Mother gave them an heirloom clock from her bottomless trunk. Daisy gave them a set of white bone china dishes with a navy-blue rim.

She came to the wedding from Kenora where she worked in the yard office and boarded with the Lofthouses. They lived on the crest of a hill overlooking the railway track. Daisy told us that when she was on the 8 a.m. shift she ran down the hill to catch a ride on the passenger train whose engine was replaced at Kenora. The old engine was detached below the hill and sent to the roundhouse which was beyond the yard office. Daisy jumped onto the cowcatcher and hung onto the grab irons that angled back to the engine. It was faster than walking to work, and more fun.

Until he went into politics in 1919, Daisy had a ride home from her evening shift with Peter Heenan, who drove a small engine from Kenora to Keewatin each night. He was a witty Irishman who had been a CPR engineer at Kenora since 1902, when it was called Rat Portage.[14]

Daisy visited Clarence and Phoebe in Dinorwic and fell in love with a framed photograph of Phoebe's soldier brother. When Archie Wright came home she won him with her lively dark eyes and tomboy vitality. They were married in September 1920, in the Anglican rectory in Dryden, and moved into a cottage high on the shore of Wabigoon Lake on a point of land that jutted out into the water and faced the village. It was only a short trip by rowboat across to Wabigoon.

Daisy, who had much to learn about cooking, boiled cornmeal one day which swelled, overflowed the pot and threatened to swamp the tiny kitchen. She wrapped the cooking pot in towels and hurried down the trail to the lake where she dumped the mess in the water, rinsed the pot and put her worst culinary failure from her mind. Archie was out, and she didn't tell him about the incident.

Daisy at twenty-one.

*The portrait of Archie Wright
Daisy fell in love with.*

The cooked cornmeal drifted in yellow patches on the bottom of the lake for weeks. It remained near shore as though to haunt her and it greatly mystified her husband. When they took the rowboat to town he always stopped rowing a short distance out and looked over the side. "I'll be darned," he'd say. "It's still there. Must be some kind of weed or fungus. Funny I never noticed it before. Have you ever seen anything like it?"

And Daisy always replied, "Never."

Soon after Daisy's marriage the CPR requested that she give up full-time work and go on call. Both she and Clarence had new responsibilities and Bert, Gray and I provided for the family. There were six of us now; Win had joined us soon after Bert came home. The invalid she had lived with was dead, and she had met no men in an England plundered by the war. In Dinorwic she took a shine to Charlie Stanford. But Charlie had a wife – in a mental hospital in Britain.

For Win, moving to the homestead after twenty-seven years in an English city was like falling down a well. Gray and I bought her a red and green Mexican parrot brought to Dinorwic by a trunk man whose wife didn't like birds. "Come back, come back!" the bird screeched when the salesman left. It also said other words never before heard in our household. Win covered the cage with a dark cloth whenever he squawked these atrocities. Finally the bird confined itself to "Pass the salt" and "Who's there?," and to a sound like that of a window being raised.

He played coy when Mother or Win was near and rubbed his topknot against the bars of his cage. This meant "Scratch my head." He loved that and would nibble their fingers with his huge beak. I tried the game one day and he made a grab for me that was anything but playful. I swiftly withdrew and Gray said, "What's the matter, you scared of pretty Joey? Mum and Win aren't afraid." Gray stuck his finger in and Joey snapped it with his beak. Gray danced like a brave at a powwow, screaming wicked words that put Joey's efforts to shame. Mother and Win looked stunned.

I expected to see Joey in a chicken stew next day but he lived on for years to entertain our mother and sister. Gray was lucky. Nobody put a bag over his head or washed his tongue with soap. He was a young man now and, in any case, had always gotten away with everything short of murder when Father wasn't around.

Win wanted a piano too. She wanted it very badly. This was like asking for the moon but Bert, Gray and I did manage to save enough to buy a second-hand piano in Dryden and have it shipped by train to Dinorwic. The day we wrestled that instrument through the door at Creekside (removing part of the door frame in the process) was one of our happiest days on the homestead. Win played by note; the rest of us discovered some ability to play by ear – except Gray, who had no interest at all in music.

The year before I joined the section gang the Hudson's Bay Company hired me as a part-time clerk. This was right up my alley. The Bay store was the hub of the community. One day an Ojibway stood in the doorway with an albino beaver in his arms. "This one's not for sale," the manager said. "It should be on display somewhere." Years later, while living in Toronto, I discovered what he had done with this rare and exotic find. On a visit to the Royal Ontario Museum, I saw the albino beaver displayed in a glass case with this inscription: CAUGHT IN DINORWIC ONTARIO AND PRESENTED BY THE HUDSON'S BAY COMPANY.

When the Ojibways were in town the men sat on the counters as though they owned the place. Women sat cross-legged on the floor. Babies were propped against the wall in tikanagans. Waiting on the Ojibway women was a challenge. They had all been to boarding-school; some had more education than I did. However, since they never used English words, I was obliged to learn some Indian vocabulary. When an Ojibway woman said *kesosewat*, I would point to all the yellow objects in the room and find perhaps that she wanted bananas. When offered the wrong thing, the customer said *kaween*, which meant no. Purchases were sometimes paid for in *basig shunia*, the Indian phrase for coins, but were more often put on the bill until furs were brought in from the trap line. The ban on the use of English was imposed to prevent the women from fraternizing with white men. Sometimes this happened anyway. Mike Zoccole, who owned the pool hall, married an Indian. He was quickly forgiven by her relatives and the Ojibway men became experts at the game of pool.

15

SHOVELS AND SHIMS

In other parts of Canada people danced the Charleston and enjoyed the prosperity of the roaring twenties. In Dinorwic, Gray and I worked on the section gang and earned about $45 each every two weeks. The pay went into Dad's cash box and he gave us a dollar each for pocket-money. Off we went to Zoccole's, where pool cost ten cents a game. We sighted along the cue rods and – click! – the balls collided and rolled down the green table. Soon our Indian friends had our dollars and, worse still, we each owed fifty cents. We didn't dare let Dad know we were gambling so the next pay-day we asked for a raise, just this once. He doled it out and somehow we lived with our guilt.

Gray had joined the section gang at sixteen; I had followed him a year later when I was fifteen. Our group worked a five-mile section of double track. The first operation of the day was track patrol, the inspection of the line for defects. Some of the road-bed in our section was muskeg, some was clay. When frost penetrated in the fall the different soil types heaved unevenly and humps formed on the rails. These varied from as little as an inch to the depth of a railroad tie. The correction process was called shimming. Shims were hardwood somewhat shingle-shaped, thicker at one end than the other, and anything from a few inches to several feet in length. The men began work some distance behind the hump and put shims under the rails, making a gradual slope to even out the track. Shimming went on all winter as frost penetrated more deeply into the road-bed.

Two or three men who had seniority did the winter work. I

was involved in removing shims in the spring. This was the worst time of all. Sections of rail that had heaved sank rapidly as the frost went out. Shims were replaced with thinner ones. This was done several times before the track was back to normal.

During the time I worked on the section, heavier locomotives came into use and heavier track had to be laid. Rails were changed from 80 pounds per yard of steel to 110 pounds per yard. Large gangs of men did several miles of line a day in the early summer. They laid the rails with the ends too close together. There was little room for expansion. The fiery sun of advancing summer heated the rails until some of them bowed sideways into what were called sun kinks.

By the time this problem appeared the men who laid the rails had moved on and the section men had to deal with it. When a rail kinked it was taken out immediately. A flagman went to stop the oncoming train. This happened so often that the engineers were furious, especially when they were stopped at MacDonald's Cut, a mile-long curving grade where the railway ran through a cut in the hills east of Dinorwic.[15] I hated being flagman. The flag was held at arm's length and the engineer, fairly spitting with rage, leaned out the cab window and tried to snatch it from me.[16]

Removing the final spikes from a rail kinked sideways required caution. When the rail was free it sprang out with great force and could smash the legs of a man standing in the wrong place. A new rail was measured and marked, then cut one blow at a time with a sledge-hammer striking a cold chisel placed on the rail. It was cut perhaps two inches short of the space. Then three or four rails on both sides of the rail taken out were moved towards the space, leaving a gap between the joints to allow for expansion. Track work was done then with elbow grease, sweat and simple tools.

The flagman posted a mile from the work site clipped a small explosive device called a torpedo to each rail, but not parallel, so that the engineer would hear two distinct reports. The flagman moved down the track and held up a red flag as the train approached. If he lowered the flag the signal was "Slow and caution for a mile." If he kept it raised the message was "Stop within the mile." Sometimes the vibration of the rails made torpedoes fall off. Gray and I collected these, clipped them to branches of a tree and exploded them with 22-rifle bullets. We worked hard but there was always a way to have some fun.

Most of the men on the gang were Italian, German or Finnish and spoke broken English. I felt particularly sorry for a new immigrant from Italy, only sixteen years old, struggling to learn section work and a completely foreign language at the same time. Some of the immigrants brought their families with them. Others came alone and didn't see their loved ones for twenty years.

The section gang returned to the tool house each day on a railway handcar, a flat conveyance propelled by a double handlebar in the centre. With twelve men on the car we hung onto each other and some of us stood on one foot.

One day when we thought the line was clear the sharp wail of a train's whistle sounded behind us. We piled off, stumbling, grabbing, getting in each other's way. If the train had hit the handcar, flying tools would have killed some of us. The car cleared the tracks a second before the train flashed by.

There were other dangers. When a harvester train whizzed past, jeering faces hung out the windows and pop bottles whistled through the air with deadly speed. I hit the ground with the rest of the gang. Twenty minutes later we dodged the fire from the second section of the train.

Some days later we worked on the curve of MacDonald's Cut where the banks were steep. It was time for revenge. Each of us cut a long thin spruce tree. When we heard the unique signal of a harvester we scrambled up the bank to the level of the train windows. Hidden by the trees, we raised our whips and the protruding heads were smacked with a force that knocked off their caps.

In the early 1920s thousands of men came through on these trains from the east to harvest grain in the west. At Ignace station they raided the luncheon stall of Mrs. McClure, a lady famous all over the division for her pies. The harvesters smashed her stall to pieces.

The boat used by Edward, Prince of Wales, during a Canadian fishing holiday was moored close to Vermilion Bay station. The harvesters pitched boulders into it. In Dinorwic they set fire to hay stacked along the CPR right-of-way by Mike Zoccole. He ran home for his shotgun; some of the harvesters were armed and returned the fire. There were no casualties, but a small hole remained in the window of Dinorwic station where a shot just missed the agent's head. And Daisy, standing on the wide top step of the Hudson's Bay store, felt a bullet whiz past her cheek and heard it thud into the building.

All the residents of railway towns were relieved when two Mounties were posted on each harvester train.

16

BUSHWHACKERS

After the First World War ended, Max and Kurt Naumann, relatives of the Eger family, came to live in our village. They showed up on the section gang wearing German uniforms. Face blanched and eyes blazing, Bert threw himself at the nearest green-suited figure. Men pulled him back and held him until the moment passed. These sudden flare-ups of Bert's lessened as time went on and later he and the Naumann boys became good friends.

Scandinavian and British people also came to homestead in Dinorwic. They built homes of unpeeled logs. Roads were cut through the bush in all directions. The provincial government passed the Statute Labour Law to help get the roads cut and kept in good condition. Each family had to do three days' work a year on the main road and maintain their private road that connected to it. For one day's work done by a settler the government paid for three more workdays. A man had the option of paying someone else to do his share of statute labour.

One of the new British settlers, Mr. Keeworth, hired Gray and me to cut pulpwood. On the first morning he said, "I'll take you to the proper area, it wouldn't do for you boys to get lost." Bundled to the ears, he looked even shorter than he was. A scarf covered his nose; his moustache bristled with icicles. With a gun under his arm and a compass in his hand he said, "Follow me!" After a few paces he consulted the compass. Held close to the gun, it spun wildly. Mr. Keeworth moved in circles for awhile, then said, "This damned compass doesn't work, we'll have to take our chances."

Gray and I cut sixteen cords of wood for him, enough to fill a boxcar. When payment came from the pulp mill in Kenora the amount was less than Keeworth owed the Hudson's Bay store, so he was unable to pay us. A tool maker by trade, he gave us a box of tools in lieu of money. "We can't eat these!" Mother said, but that was all we ever received for cutting the sixteen cords of wood.

Mr. Collier was a retired sergeant-major of the British Army. He never walked, he marched. A military moustache waxed to points accented his ruddy face. The man was overbearing and when *he* asked us to cut a carload of pulpwood, we consented.

Sometimes he came to the site to chop wood himself. He arrived with his axe on the slope of his shoulder like a rifle, marched up to a tree, ordered "Arms!," then "Stand at ease!." He stared fiercely at the tree, took one pace to the rear and with a "Ready, aim, cut!" he chopped all around the tree like a beaver. This was not the way to fell a tree and it made us nervous. We asked him which way the tree would fall so we could be out of the way. He said, "How do *I* know? I'm not a bloody prophet." From then on we kept our distance when Collier cut wood.

Once again, when the time came for us to collect, all the money had gone to pay the store bill. With the air of doing us a great favour, Mr. Collier paid us off with books from his large collection. Mother and Dad accepted this compensation with pleasure.

The winter I turned fifteen I worked with Bert and Gray in a gang chopping out a roadway that would some day be part of the Trans-Canada Highway. The old Gold Rock road ran straight south from the hotel across the railroad tracks for about a mile, then turned east into the bush. It was here that the work began. Living in tents, we worked toward the camp and then away from it so that it wasn't necessary to move often. During this bitterly cold winter, forty below zero was the rule and often the temperature dropped lower.

I awoke shivering in the pitch-black night. Two hours ago I had stoked the tin heater in the middle of the tent. It was someone else's turn now but there was always this wait while a man lay rolled in his blanket hoping that another person would rise and build up the fire.

Too soon it was time to roll from the cots and pull on heavy wool breeches, mackinaw jackets and moccasins with thick insoles. Then we rushed to the dining tent for porridge, pancakes, bacon and buckets of scalding coffee. Vast amounts of food provided the energy for wading in waist-deep snow, felling trees and keeping body temperatures close to normal. Men whipped each other's shoulders and buttocks with branches to stimulate circulation. Head down on your arms, you waited to feel the sting that would prove your blood was still flowing.

Frozen and brittle poplars often snapped and fell in the wrong direction. When they struck another tree and broke off a branch or the top, danger to the workers was increased. Nobody could move quickly in the deep snow.

"Nelson, look out!" someone yelled. Sharp as a bayonet a severed tree top plunged toward the man's head. He dodged to the side and screamed as the missile shattered his elbow.

Soon after this the woods operation was closed. The deep snow and vicious cold made it too dangerous. The building of the Trans-Canada Highway continued in fits and starts over the years.

During most winters Bert, Gray and I cut wood for the pulp-and-paper mills. They paid $5 for a cord of wood 4 x 4 x 8 feet; that is, four-foot lengths stacked. Spruce was cut in the swamp, hauled out with a team of horses and loaded into boxcars bound for Kenora or Port Arthur paper mills.

The woodcutter earned $2.00 to $2.25; the teamster, $1.50; the man who stacked the wood in the boxcar, 25 cents per cord. A dollar was held back for each cord: 50 cents by the mill until the contract was completed, and 50 cents by the government until the slash left by cutting was burned off in the spring.

The Dryden Paper Company had a different system. Their mill, located on Wabigoon Lake, used jackpine to make kraft paper. They paid $5 for the equivalent of a cord cut in 12-foot lengths and stacked on the steep banks of Dinorwic Lake. A timber scaler measured the diameter of each log. When the lakes opened in the spring the company sent a special boat called an alligator to Dinorwic to string booms of logs from the shore out into the lake. These boom logs, big enough for a man to walk on, were chained together. A cable was attached to the blocks holding the jackpine; these were jerked loose and the pile rolled down to the water. The alligator towed the chained logs back to shore to encircle the jackpine and the whole thing, called a log boom, was towed across the lake, past Wabigoon and on to Dryden.

Pulpwood cut in twelve-foot lengths for the Dryden Paper Company.

The Dryden Paper Company's alligator on Wabigoon Lake.

17

A FUTURE FOR THE BOYS

Jn Dinorwic the Hudson's Bay Company had been a monopoly for some time. This was broken briefly in 1922 by the Great Lakes Fur Trading Company,[17] which came to Dinorwic with Ed Thompson as manager. It was Ed who acquired the settlement's first radio.

It certainly brought people into the store. There was always someone attempting to tune in a station and others waiting their turn to put on the headphones and twiddle the knob. In those days one could not simply turn to a number on a dial to capture a station and enjoy clear reception. The squeals and whistles of static competed constantly with the voice or music transmitted. Still, this was a magic box. To pull sound from the air was a feat that nobody in Dinorwic completely understood.

When loudspeakers were developed a few years later Gray and I bought a second-hand earphone radio for $25 from a man in Kenora who had graduated to a set with a speaker. Our radio entertained the family for years. We took turns listening to two American stations on that small radio. One of them was located in Denver, Colorado.

As for the Great Lakes Fur Trading Company, the radio was not enough to ensure its survival beyond the 1920s. After its demise the Hudson's Bay Company regained the throne of commerce in Dinorwic.

I was at the railway station once when Taffy Jones loaded his wagon with freight for the Bay store. Prince stood quietly, now and then looking over his shoulder as a hefty box thunked into the wagon. When all was loaded the horse sat down between the shafts. Taffy kicked him a couple of times but he would not budge. "All right, you lazy bugger," Taffy screamed, "I'll move this freight by myself!" With a borrowed wheelbarrow he pushed load after load up the hill to the store. As he made the final trip Prince got up and followed him with the empty wagon. Smiling.

One summer Gray and I took a break from the section gang and worked in a sawmill at Osaquan, near Ignace. One hundred and fifty men slept in the stifling bunkhouse. Or tried to sleep. Lice travelled from bunk to bunk. The only remedy was to wash the head in coal oil.

There were two twelve-hour shifts, each of two weeks' duration. Run by steam-power, the machines had control levers. The man who oiled the pulleys could almost stand upright under the mill operation, which took place on an upper level less than six feet above the lower floor.

Safety was up to the individual. One day a piece of block fell through a hole in the floor above and jammed a pulley underneath. The millwright came down to see why the machine had stopped. Standing between the belt and a pillar, he pried the

Osaquan sawmill from the lumber pile.

block loose. The belt, moving now, caught his crowbar and then pinned him to the pillar. This stopped the machine again, so the injured man survived.

Saws of all shapes and sizes whirred like silver streaks day and night. Many workers lacked several fingers. I saw a fellow stumble and put out his hand for balance. In a second it lay on the sawdust while blood pumped from his wrist. "Let's get out of here while we're still in one piece," Gray said that night.

We went home and sat down with Bert to discuss the future. Bert had tried a number of jobs, including a short-lived bakery in Wabigoon. Our brother Clarence had progressed from clerk in the Hudson's Bay store in Dinorwic to manager for that company in Nipigon in 1923. He was currently working for a grocery company in New York and planned to return to Canada to open his own shop. We decided that we had better follow his lead if we were to get anywhere in life.

Work on the track that summer was as back-breaking as ever but now we had the dream of a business of our own. We squeezed every nickel; Zoccole's pool hall saw no more of us. Dad had agreed to our saving for the piano and now he supported this venture. A couple of years later we had a family conference. There was enough money to start our careers as capitalists in a modest way but we had no idea where to begin.

"Why not a fish-and-chip shop?" Bert suggested. This staple of the English diet was unknown in Canada, or so we thought. It was certainly a novelty in Dryden. The day we opened a group of young chaps came in prepared to gamble. "How many chips do you get for a dollar?" they asked.

The fish came from Pitt's butcher shop and we used anything he had in stock on that day. Even salmon, a rather exotic fish to pair with chips. The food was deep-fried and wrapped in waxed paper and old copies of the *Dryden Observer*. Bert baked pies and tarts; people could buy a complete take-out meal from us. The problem was that in the mid-1920s Northwestern Ontario was not ready for fast food. We had a few orders from the Red Cross Hospital but not much business from the locals once the novelty had worn off. We stuck it out as long as we could. Then Bert went to work in Merrill, Rhind and Walmsley's general store in

Wabigoon, where Clarence became a partner in 1926. In 1927 the Red Lake gold rush was in its second year and Gray and I decided that opportunity lay in the gold fields. We hoped to be part of this phase of the gold rush and perhaps do some prospecting of our own.

18

THE *DOUGLAS WRIGHT*

The Canadian National Railway (CNR) train chugged toward Hudson, a village west of Sioux Lookout. The wheels sang soon be there, soon be there. "I wonder how big the place is," Gray said.

"Must be quite a crowd there now," I said, "waiting for the ice to go out of those lakes up north where the claims are. I hope we get hired for the summer." My long legs were cramped. I stretched them across the seat where packsacks and a tent were piled.

"We should make a bundle this summer," Gray said. At the moment we had $3 between us. It was May 1927.

Visible gold had been discovered in the Red Lake area the previous year. The gold rush began in January 1926, when Dome Mines Limited optioned to purchase nineteen claims staked by Ray and Lorne Howey, at Red Lake. Hundreds of prospectors drove dog teams over frozen lakes and narrow bush trails, a journey of two weeks for many. When Dome Mines dropped their option on the Howey property in September 1926, most prospectors left the area. However, in February 1927 activity resumed at Howey mines, a shaft was sunk and gold fever blazed again. Prospectors would be hiring men to help work their claims as soon as the winter ice went out.

A fellow named Finlayson had driven us over the long, rough gravel road from Dinorwic to Quibell, located on the CNR line. Our route to Red Lake would begin at Hudson and cover a chain of lakes and rivers.

When we reached Hudson, the waters of Lost Lake sparkled on one side of the tracks. A broad steep hill rose on the other.

Canvas crowded the hill and another tent popped up like a mushroom as we watched. All were waiting for breakup so they could make a dash for the gold fields.

Hungry, we followed a stream of men to the top of the hill. Two adjoining tents housed the kitchen and dining room of Mr. Cockburn's restaurant.

"Put your tent next door, boys," he said. "And how about giving me a hand? I can't pay wages but you can have free meals instead." I waited on tables and Gray helped Roy Cruikshank, a former Toronto chef who planned to go along when Cockburn took the restaurant to Red Lake. We were pleased to have work while waiting to be snapped up by a prospecting team.

Two days after we joined his staff Mr. Cockburn received a telegram from Toronto. His son had been in an accident. He took the first train home, leaving Roy in charge with no money for supplies. This was hard on Roy, who took great pride in his profession. Soon we were reduced to serving pancakes. There was not much else but a sack of beets. Roy made beet wine. After several glasses were consumed, he gazed at the large trunk left behind by his employer.

"Maybe there's some money in that thing," he said. He broke the lock with a kick and raised the lid. "Son of a bitch! Look at this!" he said. The trunk was crammed with poker chips and decks of cards. Roy slammed down the lid. It was clear that the restaurant in Red Lake would be only a front for a gambling joint. The next day Roy sold some of the boss's equipment and bought a ticket to Toronto. We waited again to be hired by prospectors, and for transportation.

Gray and I were lucky, at least we thought we were, when we picked up another job right away working on a scow called the *Douglas Wright*.[18] Loaded with lumber from MacDougall's Mills, it was going to the Hudson's Bay post at Gold Pines[19] on the route to Red Lake. The scow was propelled by a Ford motor fitted with a heavy chain connected to a paddle-wheel at the stern. This trip would be the *Douglas Wright's* maiden voyage across Lost Lake, the connecting English River, which had two rapids, and over the rough waters of Lac Seul.

There were six on board: a captain, an engineer, and my

The Douglas Wright during the Red Lake gold rush.

brother, myself and two others as crew. The estimated time span
for the trip was one week. We spent two weeks on that scow,
harassed to the point of mutiny.

The boat crossed Lost Lake and made her way through the
rapids without difficulty. But on Lac Seul heavy waves put
intermittent stress on the chain and snapping links were a frequent
problem. The trip came to a halt each time the chain had to be
repaired. Finally, the timber was unloaded at Gold Pines.

We were almost across on the way home when the battery
died. The boat drifted into a bay and came to rest beside an island.
The engineer and captain took the canoe we carried and went to
Sioux Lookout for a new battery and provisions. Our food supply
had run out.

They said they would be back within a day. Twenty-four
hours stretched to forty-eight. Hunger gnawed at our bellies. A
small piece of bread, green with mould, lay on the floor of the
galley. I tied a bent nail to a cord and lowered the bread to the
fish swimming around the boat. A big jackfish grabbed the bait
and held on until I had him halfway up to the rail. Then our
dinner vanished with a splash and a flip of the tail. For a moment I

thought I would be pitched over the side to swim after him. Then Gray went to look for rabbits and came back with a mud turtle. With a hole drilled in its shell it was tied to a tree as insurance against starvation.

At last the engineer and captain returned in a motor boat driven by a Mountie and carrying food.

"Come on, boys," the captain ordered. "Get this stuff unloaded and fix a meal for the officer."

"Wait a minute," the Mountie said. "How long is it since you fellows have eaten?"

"Oh, about three days."

"Then cook yourselves a meal. I'm not hungry."

The smell of bacon frying drove us wild. When it was cooked along with three dozen eggs we made up for the days of privation.

On her way again, the *Douglas Wright* approached the rapids it had descended so easily. Going up was another matter. First the engineer sent a crew member to shore with one end of a rope which he secured to a large tree. The other end was wrapped several times around a capstan on the boat. Gray was stationed behind this, pulling on the tail end of the rope to keep tension on the length that stretched between tree and scow. This helped to maintain the forward motion as the *Douglas Wright* inched up the rapids.

Loose rope piled up on the deck behind Gray. Suddenly the boat slipped, then raced backward. Before the rapidly sliding rope could peel the skin from his hands, Gray let go. It snapped forward and the coils behind my brother wrapped round his body and jerked him to the deck.

"You stupid bugger!" the engineer yelled.

Now the captain decided to make use of the raft above the rapids. It had been there all along, evidently intended for use in situations like ours. Floating near the lip of the rapids, it was anchored by cables to poplar trees on each side of the river. This contraption was fitted with a winch and a cable.

The engineer and I paddled the canoe up to the raft where he left me, taking one end of my cable to the boat where he hooked it to the bow.

With the paddle-wheel at the stern, Gray pulling stoutly on

the rope that was tied to the tree, and me turning the winch, the scow crept up the rapids once more. The poplars holding my platform bucked and swayed. The raft, made of loose logs in a frame, joggled under my feet. Then my cable whipped from its drum. The heavy handle of the winch spun wildly and I fought for balance as the *Douglas Wright* sped backward one more time.

A fishing launch slipped easily up the rapids and the owner offered me a ride to Hudson. If Gray hadn't been back on that scow, I would have left the whole mess behind. But I could see the captain pounding on the cabin with his fists. I stayed on the raft.

On the next attempt we made it all the way up. No trouble was expected at the second rapids. This was a longer stretch but not as steep. The boat reached the bend in the river where the force of the water began and – bingo! – down we went again.

When part way up the second time we moved close to shore and threw a plank across. The captain and I went ashore with a rope. On a point of land stood a big tree just right for our purpose. But the rope was too short.

The captain said, "Never mind, get this piece around the tree and I'll join another one to it." I scrambled through logs and underbrush and tied my end to the tree. He joined his rope to mine and it was lying in the water as I went back up the plank.

Halfway up the rapids we lost the rope.

"You bloody idiot!" the captain screamed. "Can't you even tie a knot?"

The engineer was yelling at my brother, assuming that he had let go of his section of the rope. By this time it was dark. The boat was moored at the shore and Gray and I lay awake fuming and fighting clouds of mosquitoes.

Morning light revealed my handiwork securely tied to the tree. It was the captain's knot that had slipped.

The scow inched up the second rapids that morning and made it back to Hudson. When we cashed our pay cheques at the bank there the manager was surprised to hear that we were through with the *Douglas Wright*. "You guys aren't very good sailors," he said. I thought he was disappointed that we weren't going to open an account.

19

FIELDS OF GOLD

The 1927 spring breakup was finally over. Most of the prospectors had left for the gold fields, but we were back in Hudson with no job in sight. Fortunately, the day after our return we met two scouts from a Sudbury syndicate. They hired us on the spot to carry out trenching and blasting in the mining area of Woman Lake, east of Red Lake. Henri Lévesque was a French Canadian, Hans Heinie a German who never missed an opportunity to give orders. He said, "We're going to take the train to Sioux Lookout for supplies. Tomorrow we'll take the passenger launch across to Pine Ridge on our way to Woman Lake. Have your trunk packed first thing in the morning or we'll go without you."

With wages from the scow trip we bought fishing lines and trolls, kept enough money for the next day's meals and sent the rest home to Mother and Dad. That was a mistake. It was three days before Hans and Henri came back. Again we waited with hollow stomachs for employers to show up. A chap sitting in a fancy boat at the dock looked like a good prospect for a handout. But Joe was in the same predicament as we were. He had sold his garage business in the east to buy his boat, expecting to make a fortune hauling prospectors from Hudson to Gold Pines where they would continue the journey by canoe. His expensive craft proved to be too small and not sturdy enough for the rough waters of Lac Seul and the river rapids.

Now Joe was trying to sell his handsome, useless boat to raise money for his fare home. He joined us in the search for food. We fished for perch at the dock. They refused to bite. In the abandoned kitchen of Mr. Cockburn's restaurant we found only flour. Gray, ever the optimist, said, "I'll mix water with this and cook us some pancakes." They looked edible in the pan and smelled good. Drooling, we each bit into one and found ourselves trying to chew a good imitation of solid rubber. We rolled the pancakes into balls and played catch with them.

Hans and Henri returned whiskered, grubby and reeking of booze. Gray said, "I hope you guys had a good time while we hung around here flat broke and starving."

"Oh," said Hans, "We have an account at the hotel. You could have eaten there, but you had your own tent so we thought you were independent."

"You might have told us!" Gray said and we wasted no more time. In the hotel tent we sat down to pork chops, potatoes, gravy, corn bread and apple sauce. In spite of our vast appetites it was impossible to enjoy the food – poor Joe stood outside the window, watching every bite as it went from fork to mouth. I held up a piece of bread and pointed to my pocket. He shook his head and melted into the gathering darkness. He had gone to join the host of men who lost their shirts to gold fever. We never saw him again.

The following morning we were on our way to the gold fields at Woman Lake. The first hundred miles of our journey was by motor boat to Gold Pines, where we spent the night in a tent-hotel packed with men. They slept on two-tiered metal bunks and each brought his own blanket. This protected the hotel from theft and reduced the spread of lice.

Hans and Henri didn't know how to order food. They bought 100 pounds each of flour and sugar, boxes of raisins, a bag of beans, a slab of bacon and some oatmeal. Only the sugar would last the summer and beyond. We wondered if they were planning to make home brew.

They hired a man with two large freight canoes powered by outboard motors. The rest of the journey by water was spent in these, with two of our party towed behind in the light canoe that was needed on location. It was the crossing of nine portages that made this a trip to remember.

On these narrow trails between lakes, each man carried 150

pounds on his back. Feet slipped on spruce poles that spanned the oozing swamps. Huge rocks loomed in the middle of the trail. Every stumbling step of the way the load bowed our backs and stretched neck muscles into bands of fire.

The leather strap which supported the load extended up each side of the back and widened across the forehead so that the head and neck bore a share of the 150-pound load. During three trips across each of the nine portages we trudged with backs bent forward at the hips. The load carried at the small of the back was supported at either side with the hands.

Once Gray tripped at the top of a high rock and tumbled all the way down. His pack, which contained dynamite caps, bounced behind him. I held my breath until my brother got up, laughing.

At last we were settled at the claim site. Just our three tents were there. We had an occasional visitor when someone passed in a canoe and stopped to chat.

It was a summer of trenching, blasting, fighting blackflies and mosquitoes, and choking on the smoke from bush fires caused by prospectors burning moss from rock.

To prospect, you had to find a vein of ore. There might be an outcrop of rock with a quartz vein. Samples were taken, powdered and panned. If a trace of gold was found it was time to blast and find out how far the vein went. Perhaps a hundred yards away the vein being followed disappeared into a swamp and you had to go across to the height of land and try to pick up the vein there. If you didn't see the rock you dug trenches six feet deep to look for it. When we drilled holes for blasting we used a steel rod sharpened at the end and driven into the rock with a hammer.

The insects were a torment. We cut each other's hair down to the scalp and plastered ourselves with citronella, which promptly rolled off with our sweat. At last the sting and the itching subsided as we gained some immunity to the poison of mosquitoes and blackflies.

Our rations dwindled to beans and raisins. Game animals had left the area because of smoke from bush fires and the blasting. The trout we had enjoyed when we first arrived had gone deeper searching for cool water and we didn't have the proper equipment to catch them. We sent an order with some prospectors going to

Gold Pines, thinking that they would be there in three or four days and that our order would reach Hudson a few days after that. Doc Oakes, the pilot of the little two-seater supply plane, could fly from Hudson to our area in about an hour. So we expected our order to arrive in less than two weeks. No such luck. We waited and waited. One could hardly see across the lake for the smoke of bush fires but we listened for the engine of the supply plane. At last Hans and Henri heard of an area that was free of fire so they took the canoe and went hunting. After three days they returned with a canoe loaded with moosemeat. We stuffed ourselves for days.

Later we discovered that Doc Oakes was in Toronto conducting a lawsuit against someone who had tried to jump his mining claims.

Our last candle burned down to a puddle of wax. Determined to finish the one book we had each brought, Gray and I pushed string into jars of Vaseline and lit the ends. Crouched over the feeble flame we read for an hour or so until bedtime.

Eventually Doc Oakes's little plane landed beside our rock. We saw a protruding roll of tarpaper but almost missed the passenger. Goods were stacked on either side of him and piled from his lap to his chin. For a ride such as this, a passenger paid $1 for each pound of his body weight.

We slaved at the claim site for three months and were glad to cross the nine portages again with lighter loads. There were no written contracts in this work and men often spent a summer of labour like ours and received not a cent for it. In Gold Pines we entered the tent that housed the bank with crossed fingers. Hans and Henri didn't know if there was money in the syndicate's account after supplies had been ordered several times. However, the outfit was still solvent and we were paid $2 each per day for our work. Most of this went to pay the Rhind family's bill at the Hudson's Bay store in Dinorwic. The vision of a claim of our own and a lucky strike had long since faded from our heads.

Late that summer the Reverend Mr. Jacques, the minister serving Dinorwic, suggested that Gray and I go to Killarney, Manitoba. Friends of his, the Rigby brothers, needed men to stook and thresh grain. They each had large tracts of land and they owned a threshing-machine jointly with two other farmers. All the hired hands from each farm worked together as one threshing gang.

Gray and I had seen enough of harvester trains. We spent our savings for tickets on a regular passenger train. The grain was ready to stook when we arrived. A stook was made of a dozen sheaves standing on end and leaning in so that a point formed at the top. Gray and I had never done this, and at first every time we put one up the prairie wind blew it down.

The wind was hot; thirst was a problem. Most of the well water was full of alkali from the soil and unfit for human consumption although animals could drink it. Water was hauled in cans from a good well some distance away. Each person carried a jug with him. On the first day of stooking my brother and I ran out of water in a few hours. I walked to a farmhouse which appeared to be nearby on the rolling prairie but was actually miles away. They gave me a drink but could not spare water for me to take to Gray. When I reached him my tongue was a dry gag once more and I had nothing to give my parched brother.

One morning I saw a grain elevator and a couple of buildings that seemed to be at one end of the field. They were really eight or nine miles away in another town, concealed from view by rolling hills. These were my only experiences with the optical illusion called a mirage.

When stooking was over we threshed the grain. Each man had a team and wagon. He built a wall of sheaves around the outside of the wagon bed, threw the rest in the centre and took the grain to the thresher. The gang spent three days at one farm and then moved on to the next.

Threshers rose at daylight and stayed late in the fields, working by the headlights of Model T Fords. When at last quitting time came we relied on the hungry and thirsty horses to get us back to the farm in the darkness. There were sloughs in the area. Some covered several acres and were three feet deep. One night my team bolted into a slough. Water licked my ankles. I rammed their haunches with a pitchfork but the horses held their ground until they were satisfied. As my wagon lurched from the slough I heard the rumble of wheels and Gray's horses plunged into the water.

We were glad to go home at the end of September. The endless space of the prairies made us feel disoriented, yet Westerners could not understand how we could live hemmed in by trees.

20

THE MOVIE STAR

By now Clarence, the only Rhind with business sense, was running the Merrill, Rhind and Walmsley store in Wabigoon. After harvesting in Killarney, I occasionally worked as a clerk in the store. It was a large two-storey building on top of the hill leading to the railroad tracks. From the expanse of front window you could watch the flaming sun sink down and down to melt at last in the waters of Wabigoon Lake. You could see the eastbound train curl around the bend by the section house.

Dried apricots, prunes, peaches and raisins came off the train in wooden boxes lined with paper. Flour arrived in sacks of twenty-four, forty-nine and ninety-eight pounds. Most people bought the larger sacks, which didn't last long as bread, cake and pies came daily from the village ovens. Bags of sugar, rice and beans were opened in the store and the contents poured into metal-lined bins behind the counter. Kegs of apples scented the place, their tempting odour overpowered at clean-up time by the oily pine smell of the green cleaning compound sprinkled on the floor.

Oranges were packed in wooden crates divided in half. Two of these, standing on end and joined by a board, made a ladies' vanity table when skirted in bright cotton.

There were few cash customers. Clarence used the barter system; people who couldn't pay their accounts cut wood and cleared land for the partners. In season, they paid in blueberries. Everyone in Wabigoon had some family member picking berries daily for several weeks in the summer. What they didn't use at home went to pay for groceries.

When I was clerking I took the truck at 4 p.m. each day to the blueberry grounds north of Wabigoon to pick up berries. Some were in baskets, some in pails, some in cartons. Each person's harvest had to be kept separated until all were weighed and individual credit given. Following this procedure the berries were transferred to shipping baskets (which came knocked down and had to be assembled), then weighed once more so that the same amount filled each basket. Net covers were fastened to every unit.

Then I drove the shipment to Dryden in time for the night train to Winnipeg. The wholesalers there automatically deducted 5 per cent for spoilage. When the cheque came back our customers' accounts were credited according to the amount of berries each had contributed. Payment fluctuated as the price of the fruit rose and fell in Winnipeg. Sometimes the store received only 75 cents a basket and the pickers were convinced that we were making an unfair profit from their labour.

In reality, the store received no compensation for the work of collecting, weighing, packing and shipping the fruit, or for the bookkeeping involved. But there was no choice. This was one way to reduce the charge accounts. In a small village such as Wabigoon one did not send out dunning letters or refuse credit to anyone.

On my first day at the store, I hurried down the hill to the station with a paper bag of groceries. The train wailed as it nosed around the curve a half-mile away. There was only one stranger on the platform, a tall young lady in a dove-gray suit. Pale brown hair, firmly chiselled features, high cheekbones, gray-blue eyes — she'll still be beautiful in fifty years, I thought. "You must be Miss Rowe," I said. "I'm Eric Rhind. Mother asked me to send these things down to Creekside with you."

"Of course," she said. "I'm looking forward to the weekend with your family." She took my hand in a friendly grip, transferred the bag to her own arm and boarded the train. I went back up the hill with a curious weakness in my knees.

When I had received Mother's message that she had invited Wabigoon's new teacher for the weekend and needed eggs, bread and butter, I pictured a little old lady in black oxfords. Now I could hardly wait for the store to close. My actions were

Eric in his twenties.

automatic: pull out the bin, weigh ten pounds of sugar. Open a crate of apples, polish twenty, pile them in a basket on the counter. Write up Mr. Smith's bill. He already owes us $30. Never mind; smile anyway.

Eleven o'clock came at last and Merrill, Rhind and Walmsley closed for the night. I walked six miles down the track to Creekside. Everyone was still up. Miss Rowe was playing the piano. Mother served tea and the teacher talked of London, England, where she had lived with her parents until 1920 when they moved to London, Ontario. "From London in the smoke to London in the bush," she said, laughing. Her teeth were white as snowdrops and perfectly even. I listened, pretending to be at ease.

On Sunday Miss Rowe and I walked back to Wabigoon together. We used the track as a matter of course. At that time crushed rock was not used on the track, just sand and gravel packed level with the ties. The wide space between the two sets of rails made a comfortable path for two hikers.

Miss Rowe talked about her university days and her profession. "Tell me about life in the north, Eric," she said. Cutting pulp, prospecting, Indians, sleigh dogs, snowshoeing – it all came out in a jumbled rush. You sound like an idiot, I said to myself.

"Will you teach me to snowshoe this winter?" she asked. My heart jumped. We were friends already!

Miss Rowe spent many weekends at Creekside. "I love going to your house," she said. "It's just like visiting a home in England." On Sundays we climbed a high rock at the south end of the homestead where one could see for miles over the treetops.

Although we saw more and more of each other I still called her Miss Rowe in public. Elsie was the girl I was falling in love with; Miss Rowe was the teacher who knew French, music and city ways, all as foreign to me as the language of China. I felt like a boy with a crush on a movie star.

She boarded with the Tom Robinson family in Wabigoon. We went back to their house for tea after a hike one cold winter evening. I was ready to leave when we heard Tom pouring water into the tin washtub. Of course. It was Saturday night. The front door was sealed for the winter and solidly banked with snow. I couldn't leave without walking in on my naked host in the kitchen.

Eric watches Elsie clowning on snowshoes at Creekside.

Side by side on the couch, Elsie and I fell silent as Tom splashed in the tub. It was a long leisurely bath. The urge to kiss Elsie grew more intense but I dared not risk spoiling our friendship. If only I knew what she was thinking. When Tom plodded up the stairs to his bed I said good night and left quickly.

The chilly walk to Creekside cooled my blood but did not resolve my dilemma. I was just not good enough for Elsie.

The next time we met I shared some of my anxiety with her. "I'm only drifting through life, Elsie, what do you think I should do?"

"You're right, you *are* wasting yourself here. I know some people in Toronto. Perhaps that would be a good place to begin."

In April 1929 we waited for the eastbound train on the platform in Dinorwic. When it steamed into the station Elsie was in my arms, not caring who saw us. With our first kiss I knew there was hope, if only I could make something of myself. I had $20 to launch me in my new life.

Several times on that 1,100-mile journey to Toronto my nerve failed me. Gray and I had always gone out on jobs together, and not without prospects. For fourteen years I had lived in the bush. My skills? Working claims. Cutting pulp. Clearing land. Where I was going, no skills at all. But I was strong and healthy, there had to be something. For the hundredth time I took Elsie's picture out of my wallet. Her confident eyes looked out of the black-and-white snapshot. I coloured it in my mind. Blue-gray eyes, soft brown hair, an English complexion still rosy after nine winters in Canada. I could not let her down. She saw something in me that nobody else ever had.

At Toronto, the shell of Union Station was up and passengers used temporary wooden ramps to get around the structure. Across the street the Royal York Hotel was partly erected. There were no skyscrapers then but I felt dwarfed anyway. Clarence and Phoebe had once stayed at Mrs. Walton's boardinghouse on Strachan Avenue near the Exhibition grounds; the address was in my pocket. "Take a King or a Queen streetcar," Clarence had said. I found the place and took a room. The next morning I walked the streets looking for factories. An employment office displayed the sign "No Help Required." As I passed the Acme Screw and Gear Factory a young man washing windows called me over. "Want a job?" He gave me the inside windows to scrape free of grease and dirt. Lathes and grinders whirred close to my leg. It didn't matter. This was my first day in Toronto and already I was earning a few dollars to tide me over until I found something more promising.

The following day my employer took me to some three-storey houses built close to a ravine. This time *he* took the inside windows. I stood on a ledge with my back to a ravine that waited to snatch my falling body. After a few days I discovered that the young window washer was helping himself to portable objects in the bedrooms. I quit at once.

Day after day my feet tramped the gray pavement. Employment offices were privately owned then. One of them was taking applications. They charged a dollar to send me to a job site where the position had been filled for two days. The guys at the boardinghouse laughed. "Don't waste your money," one of them advised. "They always send half a dozen men for the same job."

A letter from Elsie renewed my courage and the St. Lawrence Market hired me to desprout potatoes. Then Elsie went to London for the summer and I hitched rides to her parents' home on weekends. "I'm helping the steam fitter at Acme Farmer's Dairy," I told her one Saturday. "I've found my trade, plumbing and steam fitting."

"Good for you Eric! I knew you'd land on your feet."

The truth was that I had landed on my rear end shortly after being hired by the dairy. My boss, the steam fitter, weighed 280 pounds, so I did all the work that required the use of ladders and the ability to worm into tight corners. Our first task on this day was to run a drainage line from the bottle-washing machine. A

Elsie and Eric at her parents' home in London, Ontario.

joint had to be made in this pipe near the ceiling over an open milk-storage tank which was 16 feet long, 8 feet wide and 5 feet deep.

We placed a wide board over this tank and lifted one end of the 10-foot long drainage pipe onto the board. Then I climbed onto the plank carrying a huge pipe wrench. The steam fitter held one end of the pipe in a hanger several feet away from the tank. I raised my end to the coupling. Crouching three feet from the ceiling, I tightened the pipe and removed the wrench.

"Give 'er another turn, Eric, and make sure we have a good connection," the boss said. So I clamped the pipe with the wrench once more and heaved with all my muscle. The wrench slipped. I tumbled from the plank and landed on my behind in two feet of milk. I clambered out and dropped to the floor. "What's so damn funny, you silly bugger," I said to the boss who was laughing so hard that his belly jiggled.

"Cleopatra! Milk baths! Ha, Ha, Ha!!" he howled, both arms wrapped around his middle, doubled over with mirth.

I was shaking with shock and fury; little white drops flew from my clothing. "What the hell do I do now?" I asked through clenched teeth.

The boss stopped laughing. "Number one," he said, "You go back in that tank and get the wrench out. Number two, button your lip or say goodbye to your job. You could be charged for a few hundred gallons of milk too."

I removed my boots and went back into the tank. When I emerged, he hosed me down and told me to dry my clothes on the hot pipes in the boiler room. "Tell the guys in there that a valve burst on a water line."

We were in the basement. All the other employees worked on the floor above. The contents of my milk bath were pumped upstairs where the fluid was sterilized, homogenized and bottled. I thought that taking my boots off the second time around was a nice gesture.

Unfortunately, I did not become an apprentice in the plumbing and steamfitting trade. The union boss told me they didn't need me. Too many men in the trade would lower wages. The greatest disappointment was that once again I had to postpone the joy of proposing to Elsie. I didn't want this wonderful girl to end up in a shack in the bush. If she married she would be fired from her teaching job and all she would have would be what I could give her.[20]

September came and weekends were hollow once more when Elsie returned to Wabigoon to teach for another year. But she promised that we would spend Christmas together in London, Ontario.

In October the stock market collapsed. I kept on pounding the pavements. A small machine shop hired me at 25 cents an hour and I found a room where I could cook on a hotplate. In the spring a letter came from Gray:

> Hi, kid how's the big city treating you. Bert is engaged to Hilda Nordstrom, getting married in June. I moved Mum, Dad and Win off the homestead to Daisy's little house on Wabigoon Lake. I'm sick of the bush myself. Coming to join you.
>
> Cheerio, Gray.
>
> P.S. Frank Hazelwood shot himself yesterday.

The Reverend Mr. Jacques, Mother, Win and Dad at Daisy's, with the village of Wabigoon in the background.

Daisy with her daughter, Hazel.

21

ENGAGED

My room was not large enough for two. When Gray arrived we searched for another one. On Sherbourne Street we found a good-sized room with two single beds and the evening meal included in the $6 each we had to pay per week. The landlady demanded her $12 in advance. We paid cheerfully, pleased with the accommodation.

I awoke at 3 a.m. with my skin on fire. Gray hit the floor at the same time and switched on the light. Dozens of bedbugs raced for cover. This was our first contact with this pest and I was thoroughly nauseated. They seemed more disgusting than lice. We examined our clothing and suitcases, then packed and went downstairs at daylight.

The landlady waited with her arms folded. "What's the idea, all that racket in the middle of the night? And just where do you think you are going?"

"Madam," I said, in my best imitation of Father at his most haughty, "You have bedbugs!"

"Never!" she said. "I have never had such a thing in my house!"

"Well, you've got them now," Gray said, "and we're leaving."

"Not till you pay me, you're not," she said, moving to bar the door.

"We've already paid you!" I said, feeling my face turn red. "Look, here's the receipt." She moved forward to snatch it from me and Gray and I bolted out the door which she had previously unlocked to bring in the milk.

She was hard on our heels, thwacking us with a large straw

broom. She was a swift runner. We escaped at the corner, dodging around a milk wagon. Perhaps she was afraid of horses.

We paused to catch our breath and have a good laugh. "Holy smoke, Eric," Gray said. "Why did we ever leave Dinorwic?"

He did odd jobs for awhile. Then he was hired by Potts Pattern Works, a small foundry. When they secured a contract with Superhealth Aluminum Cookware they hired me as a labourer. I advanced to making cookware.

"We'll be cooked to a turn ourselves before this order is finished," Gray said. Within two weeks we lost so much weight our trousers ballooned like a Dutchman's pants. We blinked sweat from our eyes and pushed on. We were paid for piece-work. When we were each making $4 a day we sent for Mum and Dad. Win stayed in Wabigoon with Daisy.

With a collection of second-hand furniture, Mum, Dad, Gray and I moved into a rented house. Once more Mum had the joy of making a home for the family. And a whole city to explore! After all those years in the bush this went to her head in the most direct manner possible. Late one Saturday she dashed into the house like a young girl. "See what I found in Eaton's basement for 25 cents!" She held out a small brown-velvet tub with a wide ribbon band of bronze silk. "Of course, it's a *winter* hat," she said wistfully. "But I can look forward to wearing it." This was the only time that Mother's habit of thrift ever failed her. She already owned a hat.

Dad said, "Put it on. Oh, my, you look smart, Lizzie."

His daily walk now had a destination: the public library. On the way, red streetcars lurched in all directions. The park with its green benches, winding paths and pink petunias was everybody's garden, kept in splendid order by persons unknown.

He prowled all the grocery stores within walking distance, sorting out bargains to carry home to Mother like trophies. They joined St. Peter's Anglican Church and soon had friends among the congregation. One was Magistrate Brown, who had once been a patrolman on the Toronto police force. Now *there* was an opportunity! Magistrate Brown interviewed me when I applied to join the force. Full of hope, I took the medical exam. The verdict was: too skinny – come back when you have some meat on your bones. I had lost fifteen pounds in the foundry. Another dream was dead. There was no chance of gaining back that weight.

Elsie, who was now teaching in Hamilton, often took the train to Toronto to visit us. When she left I would get on with her at Union Station and keep her company as far as Sunnyside, the last Toronto station. We sat on the green plush seat one day talking about Mum and Dad. "I wonder who will take care of me in *my* old age," I said.

Elsie looked into my eyes and said, "I will."

"Do you mean it?"

"Of course I do. I know why you haven't asked me to marry you, but we'll manage somehow."

The train stopped at Sunnyside. I left her with my heart pounding.

When I told them of the engagement, Mum shed a tear and hugged me. Dad said, "Well, I should hope so, after all this time."

I cut out cigarettes, walked to work, squirrelled away every penny that could be squeezed from my wages. When I had $30 I went shopping. The jeweller looked me over and pulled out a tray of cheap rings. "No," I said, handing over my money, "I want a nice one." I left the shop with a golden band set with a diamond large enough to catch the light. I longed to see it on Elsie's finger. But it would stay in the blue-velvet box until the right moment arrived.

The Depression dragged on, a stifling fog that invaded every aspect of life. Some men survived in the government work-camps established to continue the building of the Trans-Canada Highway. Thousands more, stranded in cities such as Toronto, shuffled down the lines outside the Salvation Army and Scott Mission soup-kitchens. Passing a queue of scarecrow figures with grimy skin showing through rags, I shivered. Work was slacking off at the foundry.

I joined the YMCA and became a member of the gym-leaders corps. We took evening entertainment to the homeless who were allowed to sleep on the floors of vacant factories and warehouses. Some of them came to life for a few hours and cheered the boxing and wrestling matches we staged for them. At the Y, I met Les Crane, who became a lifelong friend.

Elsie, Les and I planned a trip to Wabigoon for the summer of 1931. My friend wanted to see the woods and fields of my childhood. I wanted to give Elsie the ring in the place where our courtship began.

On the first evening in Wabigoon Les went off on a hike by himself. "Let's take a walk to the old homestead," I said to Elsie. Soon we were striding down the track as we had so often in the old days. My hand touched the velvet of the jeweller's box in my pocket. I was tempted to flash the diamond in the sunlight and put it on her finger right then.

There was nothing left of my old home by McKenzie Creek but a hole in the ground where the cellar had been. Not even a rotting board. "Let's climb the south rock for old time's sake. The view should be great on a day like this," I said. We sat close together on the little flat space at the top of the rock. Wood violets peeked from crevices. Treetops spread to the horizon. I took Elsie's left hand and slipped the ring on it. Her face paled, then flushed pink. Her eyes had a silvery shine. "Darling, did you rob a bank?" she said. I laughed and kissed her. The moment was all I had hoped for.

Gray's wedding in Toronto, 1931: Bishop Lofthouse, Eric, Mother, Gray,
Annie, Dad and Win.

Back in the city I took evening classes at Central Tech in English, Math and Foundry Practice. There were only a few days' work at the foundry now, but surely the Depression couldn't last forever.

Gray met a pretty stenographer with masses of dark waving hair. Annie McLeod was quite willing to support him till times were better. They were married at our home on September 19, 1931. Bishop Lofthouse, who had been our boxing pastor at Creekside, conducted the ceremony.[21] As he pronounced them man and wife I felt a surge of bitter envy. Mother smiled at me. Her eyes said, "Never mind, son, your turn will come."

But marriage for Elsie and me seemed further away than ever. Women teachers were fired as soon as they married. Gray and Annie moved into a couple of rented rooms. Groceries and rent for our household came to more than I could pay alone. Forced to send Mum and Dad back to Wabigoon, I myself had to return to the roominghouse. There, I once again used a hotplate for a stove and the window sill for an icebox.

Daisy, Archie and Mother at Wabigoon.

22

TILL DEATH DO US PART

When the foundry shut down, temporary jobs kept me going for awhile. One day I sat on a bread wagon pulling with all my strength on the reins. Bruce looked like a race horse and race he did. Brakes shrieked as motorists gave the horse the right-of-way. When he decided to stop he did it abruptly and sparks flew from his shoes as he clamped all four onto the pavement.

Once I returned from placing baked goods in a store to see a lady in a pretty straw hat stroking Bruce's nose. Before I could reach them he seized her hat with his lips. The hat bobbed and spittle sprayed on the brim as Bruce prepared to sink his long yellow teeth into it. I reached him in time and returned the hat with an apology. A white-faced lady stalked away holding a hat I suspected she would never wear again.

Another day a child's scream stopped me in my tracks. I raced back to the wagon. A little girl sobbed on the sidewalk. Bruce's greedy mouth was fastened to her wicker doll carriage. Again I separated the horse from his bizarre lunch. After that I looked up and down the street for possible victims before I left the wagon.

I hated garbage-collection day on my route. Bruce knocked over every available can when my back was turned and I had to pick up the trash after making a delivery. Bruce also chewed down hedges. My customers didn't appreciate the work this saved them.

I was in a Dominion Store putting in a stock of cakes when Bruce took off at a gallop up Bathurst Street. A motorist picked me up, but before we could reach him Bruce turned full tilt onto a side street. The wagon turned over and Bruce sprawled between the shafts on the roadway. He had only a few cuts but he quivered and snorted and refused to get up. A bystander went to a nearby house to telephone the company I worked for.

I sat on the wagon waiting for another horse. Smashed cherry pies bled on broken white cakes. Old Bill, our horse at Creekside, would have made short work of these. What a slow, good-natured old beast he was. Mother loved him. When he shoved his nose through the unscreened kitchen window she always gave him a lump of sugar. But one day her affection cooled more quickly than the blueberry pie she had left on the kitchen table while she went to make beds. At first she blamed her sons for the missing pie. She had no evidence, but still, we might have hidden it somewhere. Later in the day I held out a carrot to Bill. When he opened his mouth a bright blue tongue gave him away. For some time after this, when he pushed his head through the kitchen window Mother dispensed a rap on the snout instead of a lump of sugar.

The arrival of my new horse brought me back from memory lane. This animal had only one speed, low gear. He was a dull fellow compared to Bruce. When the regular driver recovered from his illness I was out of work once more.

Temporary jobs put food in my frying-pan although more and more often this was pork and beans. Each weekend I hitch-hiked to Hamilton where Elsie continued to teach. At Christmas, 1934 we were together at her parents' home in London, Ontario.

"I can't see any way out of it," I said. "I'll have to go back to Wabigoon while there is money for train fare. I hate to leave you but at least I can cut wood up there or work in the store for Clarence. We'll never be married if I stay here."

"I know you're right," she said. Her hand tightened on mine as we stared miserably at the shimmering Christmas tree in the corner.

Dad had received the old age pension in 1927; Mother had to wait until 1932 when she reached seventy. With their combined pensions and some help from their children they moved back to Toronto before I left there. Win went with them and eventually they settled in an apartment on Sackville Street where she took care of them as they aged.

Bert was working for Clarence in the store at Wabigoon; they didn't need another clerk. That winter of 1934 I was hired by a diamond-drilling company as the cook's helper. Promising veins had been discovered at Gold Rock and the mining town was coming to life.

We stayed in the bunkhouses of the old Laurentian mine and used the cookhouse. All the plaster had fallen from the log walls. It was like being in that cold house in Dinorwic where our family lived twenty years earlier. We were snowed in for the loneliest Christmas I had ever spent. Charlie Merrill, the sole freight carrier for Gold Rock, could not get in with the Christmas mail.

Later that winter I returned to Wabigoon to pound the final nails into Clarence's and Phoebe's new house. In the spring Elsie sent me a railway ticket to Toronto and met me at the station. We went on to London, Ontario, for Easter. After talking all night, we decided to get married in August. Although she would lose her job we could survive in the north.

Herb Wright (left) and Eric put the finishing touches on Clarence's house, Wabigoon, 1935.

On my return I went to the Gold Rock area with a friend to work claims owned by Clarence and Phoebe. In the summer of 1935, army worms marched through the Manitou Lakes region, stripping trees down to bare branches, carpeting the lake in green wriggle. We cooked outside the tent and often a blob of smoked caterpillars dropped from surrounding birches into the pan.

Back in Wabigoon the railway tracks writhed like serpents; trains halted on rails greasy from countless squashed bodies. That summer was part nightmare, part soaring excitement. The wedding date was August 8th and one of those trains would bring Elsie to Wabigoon, worms or no worms.

We would live in a little cabin on Clarence's place, set back amid the trees on a corner of the property. It had a kitchen, a front room with hardwood floor and one bedroom. There were no clothes closets, so I cut a hole in the bedroom wall and built an insulated cupboard. With paint and paper charged up at the store I decorated the cottage for my bride. After the living-room was papered in cream stripes with tiny roses, a letter came from Elsie suggesting that very pattern. She sent me curtains for the kitchen – snow-white with yellow ruffles all around. There was a note inside the parcel: "How about painting the kitchen to match the ruffle?" I had just finished cleaning the buttercup paint from my brush.

Three days before the wedding Elsie got off the train. She was alone. Our parents couldn't afford to make the trip. As I hurried to greet her and take her bag I remembered the young teacher I had first met on this station platform. Greta Garbo, in Wabigoon by mistake! I still found it hard to believe she would marry me and live in a cabin in the woods.

On the morning of August 8th a robin woke me, chirping his breakfast song on Clarence's and Phoebe's lawn. Rosy phlox hugged the white stones in Phoebe's garden. Traces of sunrise faded in the sky.

I stood at the head of the aisle as Elsie came through the door of the church on Clarence's arm. Her white lace dress brushed the wine-dark carpet; the broad brim of her organza hat curved around her face. Then she stood beside me. The flowers in her hand quivered slightly.

Diamond-shaped panes in the tall window behind the altar glowed amber and rose. When the minister began with "Dearly Beloved...," I knew that a dream had finally come true, the most cherished dream I had ever carried in my heart.

Eric and Elsie are wed, Wabigoon, 1935.

EPILOGUE

Eric's turn had come at last. Wedded bliss made up for the prosperous future which had failed to materialize in Canada. He and Elsie would not have met if the Rhinds had stayed in Hereford. For Eric at least, the question "Why did we come to Canada?" had been answered on a personal level.

During the winter of 1935-36 his parents were knocked down by a streetcar in Toronto and thrown across Carlton Street. They survived multiple injuries to enjoy many more years together. Mother died in 1943, and Dad in 1958 at the age of 101.

Eric's daughter, Muriel, was born in the Dryden Red Cross Hospital. Although Elsie now suffered from asthma and diabetes the baby was healthy and beautiful.

When the Second World War broke out, Bert joined the army again and was posted to a prisoner-of-war camp in Red Rock, Ontario. Life was quite comfortable for the prisoners and Bert often compared their situation with his four miserable years in Germany.

Daisy and Archie had two daughters, Hazel and Nora. During the Second World War, Daisy returned to the CPR to help relieve the wartime shortage of telegraph operators. Archie died in 1944, and Daisy stayed in Wabigoon as postmistress until 1966. In 1990 she is in her nineties and lives at Bethammi Nursing Home in Thunder Bay.

Gray remained at the foundry. He and Annie raised their three children near Toronto, and lived to a ripe old age.

Eric tried to enlist but was told that the regiment was filled by unemployed single men. In 1940 he decided to return to

Dad and Mother in Toronto.

Daisy climbs the ladder at Wabigoon station
to place a lantern on the signal board.

foundry work in Toronto, and joined the army reserve of the Royal Regiment of Canada there. Sharon Ann was born in 1942, another pink and white beauty who seemed as healthy as the first. But this baby had a defective heart valve and lived only three weeks.

Eric, Elsie and Muriel lived in Scarborough from 1950 until Elsie's sudden death twelve years later. In time, Eric found another love, Terry Drake. The couple celebrated their silver wedding anniversary in 1989.

Eric and Terry travelled to Hereford in 1988 and visited Eric's boyhood home. The old house had changed very little.

The same cannot be said for Creekside, the homestead that summoned memories just as bitter-sweet as those of Hereford. Neglected for years, the site in 1988 was brilliant with Indian paintbrush and dogbane with nodding pink bells. Fields nearby were still cleared. The house was gone; just a hole in the ground remained, with visible ridges where walls once stood. And, near the empty hole, gooseberry bushes and pink clover and poppies not yet blooming. Buttercups trailed like a yellow scarf across the field.

Dry weather had prevailed for months and the creek had shrunk to a muddy ribbon. The stone bridge under the railway track looked just as it did in the old Rhind photo album.

A train hooted at the bend and flashed by on the westbound track. Trains don't stop at Dinorwic any more. Computers program their passage over continuous welded rail. Who, nowadays, can hitch a ride on a locomotive? Or have lunch in the caboose? Who depends on a telegraph key and a prayer? Or entertains the minister between trains? Each era has its own rhythms. It was yesterday's Dinorwic that moulded Eric's life. He found fun and excitement within the drudgery and boredom of his everyday world, and this is a gift that transcends time.

The railway bridge at Creekside.

RECOMMENDED READING

Barr, Elinor and Dyck, Betty. *Ignace: A Saga of the Shield* (Winnipeg, 1979).

Bray, Matt and Epp, Ernie, eds. *A Vast and Magnificent Land: An Illustrated History of Northern Ontario* (Thunder Bay, 1984).

Collins, Ken. *Oatmeal and Eaton's Catalogue: Memoirs of an Immigrant and Life in the Roaring Twenties and the Hungry Thirties* (Dryden, 1982).

Ferguson, William. *Yesterday: A Nostalgic Glimpse As Seen Through the Sketches of William Ferguson* (Cobalt, 1979).

Parrott, D. F. *The Red Lake Gold Rush* (Thunder Bay, 1976).

Richthammer, John, Jr. *The End of the Road: A History of the Red Lake District* (Red Lake Bicentennial Committee, 1985).

Thunder Bay Historical Museum Society. *Into the New Century: Thunder Bay, 1900 – 1914* (Thunder Bay, 1989).

Wabigoon Historical Society. *Rock, Fur, Forest, Lakes: A History of Wabigoon, Dinorwic, Dyment, Gold Rock* (Wabigoon, 1988).

Wice, George. *Carved from the Wilderness: The Intriguing Story of Dryden* (Dryden, 1967).

NOTES

1. Diary of William Clarence Baikie Rhind, "Voyage to New Zealand 1878-1883," April 16, 1883.
2. King William IV reigned from 1830 to 1837.
3. Information about Interocean Park can be found in *Fort William Industrial and Commercial Review*, (1913), p. 71, and in an advertisement published in the autumn number of the *Evening Chronicle* (Port Arthur, Canada), October, 1913.
4. The trolley ran only on Central Avenue, possibly because of the golf course.
5. Hillcrest Park, in 1914 called simply Hill Park.
6. The community of Gold Rock serviced the Manitou Lakes mining area from 1890 to 1910, and again in the 1930s. Transportation was south from Dinorwic via Dinorwic Lake, a series of other lakes and a government road. A minor boom continued until about 1912. The Laurentian, Big Master and Twentieth Century mines accounted for most of the production.
7. The Grand Trunk Pacific Railway ran from the Lakehead northwestward to Superior Junction, where it joined the National Transcontinental Railway near Sioux Lookout. The NTR, built over the years from 1909 to 1912, ran parallel to the CPR line. The GTP's construction continued sporadically from 1906 to 1911, with men and supplies transported north from Ignace and Dinorwic by water routes and by winter road. In 1914 the line along with the NTR became part of the Canadian National Railway system.
8. The Wabigoon Reserve on Dinorwic Lake, #27, was surveyed in 1877 as part of the allotment set aside for the Flour and Eagle Lake Band. The word Flour refers to Wabigoon.
9. The man in charge of the pumphouse that fed water to the tank supplying the steam engines.
10. Canon Lofthouse later became bishop of Keewatin.
11. Prohibition in Ontario lasted from 1916 to 1927.
12. The Mounted Police in Kenora were Dinorwic's only contact with law and order.
13. To drop the signal, you unclipped the chain and let the weight of the falling board pull it down. Then the red signal showed. To go to green, the

operator pulled the chain. It was done this way so that if anything happened to the chain, the signal would stay red.

14. Peter Heenan was elected to the Ontario legislature as a Labour member in 1919. In 1926 he was appointed minister of labour in the federal cabinet of Mackenzie King.
15. At Brulé.
16. Engines were lower then and therefore closer to the level of the flagman.
17. The Great Lakes Fur Trading Company Limited was a short-lived venture of the 1920s, based in Northwestern Ontario.
18. Douglas Wright was an engineer with Dome Mines Limited until 1926, then associated with the Howey gold mines.
19. In 1927, Gold Pines was called Pine Ridge.
20. In those days, husbands were expected to be a family's sole breadwinner.
21. He was in Toronto for a synod meeting.

INDEX

ABOUT THE AUTHOR

Hazel Fulford became a bookworm the day she learned to read in a one-room school in Wabigoon, Ontario. By 1981 her daughters were grown, and she had completed a university degree and several creative writing courses. She began to write articles and short stories for publication and for readings. This is her first book.

Photo: Bill Lindsay

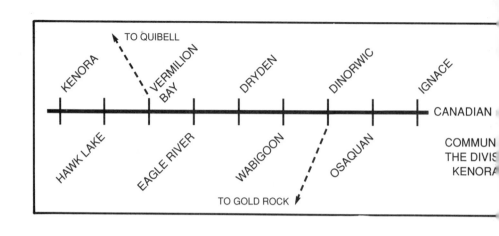

TO QUIBELL

KENORA VERMILION BAY DRYDEN DINORWIC IGNACE

CANADIAN

HAWK LAKE EAGLE RIVER WABIGOON OSAQUAN

COMMUN
THE DIVIS
KENORA

TO GOLD ROCK

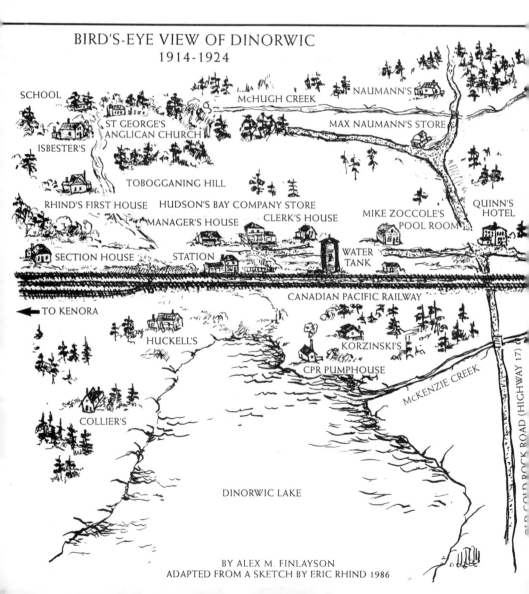

BIRD'S-EYE VIEW OF DINORWIC
1914-1924

SCHOOL

McHUGH CREEK NAUMANN'S

ST GEORGE'S
ANGLICAN CHURCH

MAX NAUMANN'S STORE

ISBESTER'S

TOBOGGANING HILL

QUINN'S
HOTEL

RHIND'S FIRST HOUSE HUDSON'S BAY COMPANY STORE

MIKE ZOCCOLE'S
POOL ROOM

MANAGER'S HOUSE CLERK'S HOUSE

SECTION HOUSE STATION WATER
TANK

CANADIAN PACIFIC RAILWAY

← TO KENORA

HUCKELL'S

KORZINSKI'S

CPR PUMPHOUSE McKENZIE CREEK

COLLIER'S

OLD GOLD ROCK ROAD (HIGHWAY 17)

DINORWIC LAKE

BY ALEX M. FINLAYSON
ADAPTED FROM A SKETCH BY ERIC RHIND 1986